FACING

YOUR

GIANTS

ALSO BY MAX LUCADO

INSPIRATIONAL
3:16
A Gentle Thunder
A Love Worth Giving
And the Angels Were Silent
Come Thirsty
Cure for the Common Life
God Came Near
God's Story, Your Story
Grace
Great Day Every Day
Fearless
He Chose the Nails
He Still Moves Stones
In the Eye of the Storm
In the Grip of Grace
It's Not About Me
Just Like Jesus
Max on Life
Next Door Savior
No Wonder They Call Him the Savior
On the Anvil
Outlive Your Life
Six Hours One Friday
The Applause of Heaven
The Great House of God
Traveling Light
When Christ Comes
When God Whispers Your Name

FICTION
Christmas Stories

BIBLES (GENERAL EDITOR)
Grace for the Moment Daily Bible
The Lucado Life Lessons Study Bible
Children's Daily Devotional Bible

CHILDREN'S BOOKS
A Max Lucado Children's Treasury
Do You Know I Love You, God?

*Grace for the Moment: 365
Devotions for Kids*
God Forgives Me, and I Forgive You
God Listens When I Pray
Hermie, a Common Caterpillar
Just in Case You Ever Wonder
One Hand, Two Hands
The Crippled Lamb
The Oak Inside the Acorn
The Tallest of Smalls
Thank You, God, for Blessing Me
Thank You, God, for Loving Me
You Are Mine
You Are Special

YOUNG ADULT BOOKS
3:16
It's Not About Me
Make Every Day Count
You Were Made to Make a Difference
Wild Grace

GIFT BOOKS
Fear Not Promise Book
For These Tough Times
God Thinks You're Wonderful
Grace for the Moment
*Grace for the Moment Morning
and Evening*
Grace Happens Here
His Name Is Jesus
Let the Journey Begin
Live Loved
Mocha with Max
One Incredible Moment
Safe in the Shepherd's Arms
This Is Love
You Changed My Life

FACING YOUR GIANTS

MAX LUCADO

A David and Goliath Story

for Everyday People

THOMAS NELSON
Since 1798

NASHVILLE   DALLAS   MEXICO CITY   RIO DE JANEIRO

Published in Nashville, Tennessee, by Thomas Nelson.
Thomas Nelson is a registered trademark of Thomas Nelson, Inc.

Thomas Nelson, Inc. titles may be purchased in bulk for educational, business, fund-raising,
or sales promotional use. For information, please e-mail SpecialMarkets@ThomasNelson.com.

Unless otherwise noted, Scripture quotations are taken from the New King James Version®. © 1982
by Thomas Nelson, Inc. Used by permission. All rights reserved.

Other Scripture references are from the following sources:
The American Standard Version (ASV). God's Word (GOD's WORD) is a copyrighted work of God's
Word to the Nations Bible Society. Quotations are used by permission. © 1995 by God's Word to the
Nations Bible Society. All rights reserved. *The Good News Bible: The Bible in Today's English Version* (TEV)
© 1992 by the American Bible Society. King James Version of the Bible (KJV). *The Living Bible* (TLB), ©
1971 by Tyndale House Publishers, Wheaton, Ill. Used by permission. *The Message* (MSG),
© 1993. Used by permission of NavPress Publishing Group. New American Standard Bible (NASB), © 1960,
1977, 1995 by The Lockman Foundation. New Century Version® (NCV), © 2005 by Thomas Nelson, Inc.
Used by permission. All rights reserved. Holy Bible, New International Version®, NIV® (NIV). © 1973,
1978, 1984 by Biblica Inc. Used by permission of Zondervan. All rights reserved worldwide. Holy Bible,
New Living Translation (NLT), © 1996. Used by permission of Tyndale House Publishers, Inc.,
Wheaton, Illinois 60189. All rights reserved. New Revised Standard Version Bible (NRSV), © 1989 by
the Division of Christian Education of the National Council of the Churches of Christ in the USA.
J. B. Phillips: The New Testament in Modern English, Revised Edition (PHILLIPS). © J. B. Phillips 1958, 1960,
1972. Used by permission of Macmillan Publishing Co., Inc.

978-0-8499-2102-5 (trade paper)

Library of Congress Cataloging-in-Publication Data
Lucado, Max.
Facing your giants / Max Lucado.
p. cm.
Includes bibliographical references and index.
ISBN 978-0-8499-0181-2
ISBN 978-0-8499-9149-3 (International Edition)
ISBN 978-0-8811-3350-9 (Spanish Edition)
1. David, King of Israel. 2. Goliath (Biblical giant) 3. Christian life. 4. Spirituality. I. Title.
BS580.D3L83 2006
222'.4092—dc22
2006019176

Printed in the United States of America

13 14 15 16 17 RRD 30 29 28 27

Denalyn and I gladly dedicate this volume to
Rod and Tina Chisholm—
faithful, dependable, and joyful servants.
We thank God for more than two decades of friendship.

CONTENTS

Contents

ACKNOWLEDGMENTS

The list of people who midwifed this book is long. Each deserves a standing ovation and early retirement.

Editors Liz Heaney and Karen Hill. When it comes to prompting thick-headed authors, you wrote the book.

Steve and Cheryl Green. If the country had overseers like you, we'd all sleep better. Thank you for your million and one acts of service.

David Moberg and the W team. The highest standard of publishing.

Susan Ligon. Your devotion to detail is exceeded only by your devotion to Christ. I'm grateful.

Sam Moore, Mike Hyatt, and the Thomas Nelson family. If a better team exists, I've not seen it.

Acknowledgments

The Oak Hills ministers, staff, and elders. May you continue to be a home for every heart.

The UpWords family of Becky, Margaret, and Tina. What gifts you have and gifts you are!

Eugene Peterson. Each reading of your books touches me. *Leap Over a Wall* changed me. Where my words sound too much like yours, forgive me—you get the credit.

Carol Bartley. Scotland Yard should have such a sleuth. I stand in awe of your editorial skills.

Steve Halliday. Thanks for another insightful Study Guide.

David Treat. Your prayers winged these words to heaven.

My three daughters, Jenna, Andrea, and Sara. Every day more beautiful. Every day more godly.

And to Denalyn. If there's a law limiting a husband's love for his wife, you'll have to visit me in prison. After twenty-five years, I'm still starstruck by you.

As Goliath moved closer to attack,
David quickly ran out to meet him.

—1 Samuel 17:48 (NLT)

1

FACING YOUR GIANTS

THE SLENDER, beardless boy kneels by the brook. Mud mois-
tens his knees. Bubbling water cools his hand. Were he to
notice, he could study his handsome features in the water. Hair the
color of copper. Tanned, sanguine skin and eyes that steal the breath
of Hebrew maidens. He searches not for his reflection, however, but
for rocks. Stones. Smooth stones. The kind that stack neatly in a
shepherd's pouch, rest flush against a shepherd's leather sling. Flat
rocks that balance heavy on the palm and missile with comet-crash-
ing force into the head of a lion, a bear, or, in this case, a giant.

Goliath stares down from the hillside. Only disbelief keeps him
from laughing. He and his Philistine herd have rendered their half of
the valley into a forest of spears; a growling, bloodthirsty gang of
hoodlums boasting do-rags, BO, and barbed-wire tattoos. Goliath

towers above them all: nine feet, nine inches tall in his stocking feet, wearing 125 pounds of armor, and snarling like the main contender at the World Wide Wrestling Federation championship night. He wears a size-20 collar, a 101/2 hat, and a 56-inch belt. His biceps burst, thigh muscles ripple, and boasts belch through the canyon. "This day I defy the ranks of Israel! Give me a man and let us fight each other" (1 Sam. 17:10 NIV). *Who will go mano a mano conmigo? Give me your best shot.*

No Hebrew volunteers. Until today. Until David.

David just showed up this morning. He clocked out of sheep watching to deliver bread and cheese to his brothers on the battle-front. That's where David hears Goliath defying God, and that's when David makes his decision. Then he takes his staff in his hand, and he chooses for himself five smooth stones from the brook and puts them in a shepherd's bag, in a pouch that he has, and his sling is in his hand. And he draws near to the Philistine (17:40).[1]

Goliath scoffs at the kid, nicknames him Twiggy. "Am I a dog, that you come to me with sticks?" (17:43 NASB). Skinny, scrawny David. Bulky, brutish Goliath. The toothpick versus the tornado. The minibike attacking the eighteen-wheeler. The toy poodle taking on the rottweiler. What odds do you give David against his giant?

Better odds, perhaps, than you give yourself against yours.

Your Goliath doesn't carry sword or shield; he brandishes blades of unemployment, abandonment, sexual abuse, or depression. Your giant doesn't parade up and down the hills of Elah; he prances through your office, your bedroom, your classroom. He brings bills you can't pay, grades you can't make, people you can't please, whiskey you can't resist, pornography you can't refuse, a career you can't escape, a past you can't shake, and a future you can't face.

You know well the roar of Goliath.

David faced one who foghorned his challenges morning and night. "For forty days, twice a day, morning and evening, the Philistine giant strutted in front of the Israelite army" (17:16 NLT). Yours does the same. First thought of the morning, last worry of the night—your Goliath dominates your day and infiltrates your joy.

First thought of the morning, last worry of the night— your Goliath dominates your day, and infiltrates your joy.

How long has he stalked you? Goliath's family was an ancient foe of the Israelites. Joshua drove them out of the Promised Land three hundred years earlier. He destroyed everyone except the residents of three cities: Gaza, Gath, and Ashdod. Gath bred giants like Yosemite grows sequoias. Guess where Goliath was raised. See the G on his letter jacket? Gath High School. His ancestors were to Hebrews what pirates were to Her Majesty's navy.

Saul's soldiers saw Goliath and mumbled, "Not again. My dad fought his dad. My granddad fought his granddad."

You've groaned similar words. "I'm becoming a workaholic, just like my father." "Divorce streaks through our family tree like oak wilt." "My mom couldn't keep a friend either. Is this ever going to stop?"

Goliath: the long-standing bully of the valley. Tougher than a two-dollar steak. More snarls than twin Dobermans. He awaits you

3

in the morning, torments you at night. He stalked your ancestors and now looms over you. He blocks the sun and leaves you standing in the shadow of a doubt. "When Saul and his troops heard the Philistine's challenge, they were terrified and lost all hope" (17:11 MSG).

But what am I telling you? You know Goliath. You recognize his walk and wince at his talk. You've seen your Godzilla. The question is, is he all you see? You know his voice—but is it all you hear? David saw and heard more. Read the first words he spoke, not just in the battle, but in the Bible: "David asked the men standing near him, 'What will be done for the man who kills this Philistine and removes this disgrace from Israel? Who is this uncircumcised Philistine that he should defy the armies of the living God?'" (17:26 NIV).

You've seen your Godzilla.
The question is, is he all you see?

David shows up discussing God. The soldiers mentioned nothing about him, the brothers never spoke his name, but David takes one step onto the stage and raises the subject of the living God. He does the same with King Saul: no chitchat about the battle or questions about the odds. Just a God-birthed announcement: "The Lord, who delivered me from the paw of the lion and from the paw of the bear, He will deliver me from the hand of this Philistine" (17:37).

He continues the theme with Goliath. When the giant mocks David, the shepherd boy replies:

You come against me with sword and spear and javelin, but I come against you in the name of the Lord Almighty, the God of the armies of Israel, whom you have defied. This day the Lord will hand you over to me, and I'll strike you down and cut off your head. Today I will give the carcasses of the Philistine army to the birds of the air and the beasts of the earth, and the whole world will know that there is a God in Israel. All those gathered here will know that it is not by sword or spear that the Lord saves; for the battle is the Lord's, and he will give all of you into our hands. (17:45–47 NIV)

No one else discusses God. David discusses no one else but God.

A subplot appears in the story. More than "David versus Goliath," this is "God-focus versus giant-focus."

David sees what others don't and refuses to see what others do. All eyes, except David's, fall on the brutal, hate-breathing hulk. All compasses, sans David's, are set on the polestar of the Philistine. All journals, but David's, describe day after day in the land of the Neanderthal. The people know his taunts, demands, size, and strut. They have majored in Goliath.

David majors in God. He sees the giant, mind you; he just sees God more so. Look carefully at David's battle cry: "You come to me with a sword, with a spear, and with a javelin. But I come to you in the name of the Lord of hosts, the God of the armies of Israel" (17:45).

Note the plural noun—*armies* of Israel. Armies? The common observer sees only one army of Israel. Not David. He sees the Allies on D-day: platoons of angels and infantries of saints, the weapons of the wind and the forces of the earth. God could pellet the enemy with hail as he did for Moses, collapse walls as he did for Joshua, stir thunder as he did for Samuel.[2]

David sees the armies of God. And because he does, David hurries and runs toward the army to meet the Philistine (17:48).[3]

David's brothers cover their eyes, both in fear and embarrassment. Saul sighs as the young Hebrew races to certain death. Goliath throws back his head in laughter, just enough to shift his helmet and expose a square inch of forehead flesh. David spots the target and seizes the moment. The sound of the swirling sling is the only sound in the valley. Ssshhhww. Ssshhhww. Ssshhhww. The stone torpedoes through the air and into the skull; Goliath's eyes cross and legs buckle. He crumples to the ground and dies. David runs over and yanks Goliath's sword from its sheath, shish-kebabs the Philistine, and cuts off his head.

You might say that David knew how to get *a head* of his giant.

When was the last time you did the same? How long since you ran toward your challenge? We tend to retreat, duck behind a desk of work or crawl into a nightclub of distraction or a bed of forbidden love. For a moment, a day, or a year, we feel safe, insulated, anesthetized, but then the work runs out, the liquor wears off, or the lover leaves, and we hear Goliath again. Booming. Bombastic.

Try a different tack. Rush your giant with a God-saturated soul. *Giant of divorce, you aren't entering my home! Giant of depression? It may take a lifetime, but you won't conquer me. Giant of alcohol, bigotry, child abuse, insecurity . . . you're going down.* How long since you loaded your sling and took a swing at your giant?

Too long, you say? Then David is your model. God called him "a man after my own heart" (Acts 13:22 NIV). He gave the appellation to no one else. Not Abraham or Moses or Joseph. He called Paul an apostle, John his beloved, but neither was tagged a man after God's own heart.

Rush your giant with a God-saturated soul.

One might read David's story and wonder what God saw in him. The fellow fell as often as he stood, stumbled as often as he conquered. He stared down Goliath, yet ogled at Bathsheba; defied God-mockers in the valley, yet joined them in the wilderness. An Eagle Scout one day. Chumming with the Mafia the next. He could lead armies but couldn't manage a family. Raging David. Weeping David. Bloodthirsty. God-hungry. Eight wives. One God.

A man after God's own heart? That God saw him as such gives hope to us all. David's life has little to offer the unstained saint. Straight-A souls find David's story disappointing. The rest of us find it reassuring. We ride the same roller coaster. We alternate between swan dives and belly flops, soufflés and burnt toast.

In David's good moments, no one was better. In his bad moments, could one be worse? The heart God loved was a checkered one.

We need David's story. Giants lurk in our neighborhoods. Rejection. Failure. Revenge. Remorse. Our struggles read like a prizefighter's itinerary:

- "In the main event, we have Joe the Decent Guy versus the fraternity from *Animal House.*"

- "Weighing in at 110 pounds, Elizabeth the Checkout Girl will go toe to toe with Jerks who Take and Break Her Heart."
- "In this corner, the tenuous marriage of Jason and Patricia. In the opposing corner, the challenger from the state of confusion, the home breaker named Distrust."

Giants. We must face them. Yet we need not face them alone. Focus first, and most, on God. The times David did, giants fell. The days he didn't, David did.

Test this theory with an open Bible. Read 1 Samuel 17 and list the observations David made regarding Goliath.

I find only two. One statement to Saul about Goliath (v. 36). And one to Goliath's face: "Who is this uncircumcised Philistine that he should defy the armies of the living God?" (v. 26 NIV).

Giants. We must face them.
Yet we need not face them alone.

That's it. Two Goliath-related comments (and tacky ones at that) and no questions. No inquiries about Goliath's skill, age, social standing, or IQ. David asks nothing about the weight of the spear, the size of the shield, or the meaning of the skull and crossbones tattooed on the giant's bicep. David gives no thought to the diplodocus on the hill. Zilch.

But he gives much thought to God. Read David's words again, this time underlining his references to his Lord.

"The armies of *the living God*" (v. 26).

"The armies of *the living God*" (v. 36).

"*The Lord* of hosts, the God of the armies of Israel" (v. 45).

"*The Lord* will deliver you into my hand . . . that all the earth may know that *there is a God* in Israel" (v. 46).

Are you four times as likely to describe the strength of God as you are the demands of your day?

"*The Lord* does not save with sword and spear; for *the battle is the Lord*'s, and *He will give you into our hands*" (v. 47).[4]

I count nine references. God-thoughts outnumber Goliath-thoughts nine to two. How does this ratio compare with yours? Do you ponder God's grace four times as much as you ponder your guilt? Is your list of blessings four times as long as your list of complaints? Is your mental file of hope four times as thick as your mental file of dread? Are you four times as likely to describe the strength of God as you are the demands of your day?

No? Then David is your man.

Some note the absence of miracles in his story. No Red Sea openings, chariots flaming, or dead Lazaruses walking. No miracles.

But there is one. David is one. A rough-edged walking wonder of God who neon-lights this truth:

> *Focus on giants—you stumble.*
> *Focus on God—your giants tumble.*

Lift your eyes, giant-slayer. The God who made a miracle out of David stands ready to make one out of you.

9

2

SILENT PHONES

OTHER EVENTS of my sixth-grade year blur into fog. I don't remember my grades or family holiday plans. I can't tell you the name of the brown-haired girl I liked or the principal of the school. But that spring evening in 1967? Crystal clear.

I'm seated in my parents' bedroom. Dinner conversation floats down the hallway. We have guests, but I asked to leave the table. Mom has made pie, but I passed on dessert. Not sociable. No appetite. Who has time for chitchat or pastry at such a time?

I need to focus on the phone.

I'd expected the call before the meal. It hadn't come. I'd listened for the ring during the meal. It hadn't rung. Now I'm staring at the phone like a dog at a bone, hoping a Little League coach will tell me I've made his baseball team.

I'm sitting on the bed, my glove at my side. I can hear my buddies playing out in the street. I don't care. All that matters is the phone. I want it to ring.

It doesn't.

The guests leave. I help clean the dishes and finish my homework. Dad pats me on the back. Mom says kind words. Bedtime draws near. And the phone never rings. It sits in silence. Painful silence.

In the great scheme of things, not making a baseball team matters little. But twelve- year-olds can't see the great scheme of things, and it was a big deal, and all I could think about was what I would say when schoolmates asked which team had picked me.

You know the feeling. The phone didn't ring for you either. In a much grander scheme of things, it didn't. When you applied for the job or the club, tried to make up or get help . . . the call never came. You know the pain of a no call. We all do.

You know the pain of a no call. We all do.

We've coined phrases for the moment. He was left "holding the bag." She was left "standing at the altar." They were left "out in the cold." Or—my favorite—"he is out taking care of the sheep." Such was the case with David.

His story begins, not on the battlefield with Goliath, but on the ancient hillsides of Israel as a silver-bearded priest ambles down a narrow trail. A heifer lumbers behind him. Bethlehem lies before him. Anxiety brews within him. Farmers in their fields notice his presence. Those who know his face whisper his name. Those who hear the name turn to stare at his face.

"Samuel?" God's chosen priest. Mothered by Hannah. Mentored by Eli. Called by God. When the sons of Eli turned sour, young Samuel stepped forward. When Israel needed spiritual focus, Samuel provided it. When Israel wanted a king, Samuel anointed one . . . Saul.

The very name causes Samuel to groan. *Saul. Tall Saul. Strong Saul. The Israelites wanted a king, so we have a king. They wanted a leader, so we have . . . a louse.* Samuel glances from side to side, fearful that he may have spoken aloud what he intended only to think.

No one hears him. He's safe . . . as safe as you can be during the reign of a king gone manic. Saul's heart is growing harder, his eyes even wilder. He isn't the king he used to be. In God's eyes, he isn't even king anymore. The Lord says to Samuel:

> How long will you continue to feel sorry for Saul? I have rejected him as king of Israel. Fill your container with olive oil and go. I am sending you to Jesse who lives in Bethlehem, because I have chosen one of his sons to be king. (1 Sam. 16:1 NCV)

And so Samuel walks the trail toward Bethlehem. His stomach churns and thoughts race. It's hazardous to anoint a king when Israel already has one. Yet it's more hazardous to live with no leader in such explosive times.

One thousand BC was a bad era for this ramshackle collection of tribes called Israel. Joshua and Moses were history-class heroes. Three centuries of spiritual winter had frozen people's faith. One writer described the days between Joshua and Samuel with this terse sentence: "In those days Israel did not have a king. Everyone did what seemed right" (Judg. 21:25 NCV). Corruption fueled disruption. Immorality sired brutality. The people had demanded a king—but rather than save the ship, Saul had nearly sunk it. Israel's first monarch turned out to be a psychotic blunderer.

And then there were the Philistines: a warring, bloodthirsty, giant-breeding people, who monopolized iron and blacksmithing. They were grizzlies; Hebrews were salmon. Philistines built cities; Hebrews huddled in tribes and tents. Philistines forged iron weapons; Hebrews fought with crude slings and arrows. Philistines thundered in flashing chariots; Israelites retaliated with farm tools and knives. Why, in one battle the entire Hebrew army owned only two swords—one for Saul and one for his son Jonathan (1 Sam. 13:22).

Corruption from within. Danger from without. Saul was weak. The nation, weaker. What did God do? He did what no one imagined. He issued a surprise invitation to the nobody from Nowheresville.

He dispatched Samuel to Red Eye, Minnesota. Not really. He sent the priest to Sawgrass, Mississippi. No, not exactly. He gave Samuel a bus ticket to Muleshoe, Texas.

Okay, he didn't do that either. But he might as well have. The Bethlehem of Samuel's day equaled the Red Eye, Sawgrass, or Muleshoe of ours: a sleepy village that time had forgotten, nestled in the foothills some six miles south of Jerusalem. Bethlehem sat two thousand feet above the Mediterranean, looking down on gentle, green hills that flattened into gaunt, rugged pastureland. Ruth would know this hamlet. Jesus would issue his first cry beneath Bethlehem's sky.

But a thousand years before there will be a babe in a manger, Samuel enters the village, pulling a heifer. His arrival turns the heads of the citizens. Prophets don't visit Bethlehem. Has he come to chastise someone or hide somewhere? Neither, the stoop-shouldered priest assures. He has come to sacrifice the animal to God and invites the elders and Jesse and his sons to join him.

The scene has a dog-show feel to it. Samuel examines the boys one at a time like canines on leashes, more than once ready to give the blue ribbon, but each time God stops him.

Eliab, the oldest, seems the logical choice. Envision him as the village Casanova: wavy haired, strong jawed. He wears tight jeans and has a piano-keyboard smile. *This is the guy,* Samuel thinks.

"Wrong," God says.

Abinadab enters as brother and contestant number two. You'd think a *GQ* model had just walked in. Italian suit. Alligator-skin shoes. Jet-black, oiled-back hair. Want a classy king? Abinadab has the bling-bling.

God does not see the same way people see.
People look at the outside of a person, but the Lord looks
at the heart (1 Samuel 16:7 NCV).

God's not into classy. Samuel asks for brother number three, Shammah. He's bookish, studious. Could use a charisma transplant but busting with brains. Has a degree from State University and his eyes on a postgraduate program in Egypt. Jesse whispers to Samuel, "Valedictorian of Bethlehem High."

Samuel is impressed, but God isn't. He reminds the priest, "God does not see the same way people see. People look at the outside of a person, but the Lord looks at the heart" (1 Sam. 16:7 NCV).

Seven sons pass. Seven sons fail. The procession comes to a halt.

Samuel counts the siblings: one, two, three, four, five, six, seven. "Jesse, don't you have eight sons?" A similar question caused Cinderella's stepmother to squirm. Jesse likely did the same. "I still have the youngest son. He is out taking care of the sheep" (16:11 NCV).

The Hebrew word for "youngest son" is *haqqaton*. It implies more than age; it suggests rank. The *haqqaton* was more than the youngest brother; he was the *little* brother—the runt, the hobbit, the "bay-ay-ay-bee."

Sheep watching fits the family *haqqaton*. Put the boy where he can't cause trouble. Leave him with woolly heads and open skies.

And that's where we find David, in the pasture with the flock. Scripture dedicates sixty-six chapters to his story, more than anyone else in the Bible outside of Jesus. The New Testament mentions his name fifty-nine times. He will establish and inhabit the world's most famous city, Jerusalem. The Son of God will be called the Son of David. The greatest psalms will flow from his pen. We'll call him king, warrior, minstrel, and giant-killer. But today he's not even included in the family meeting; he's just a forgotten, uncredentialed kid, performing a menial task in a map-dot town.

What caused God to pick him? We want to know. We really want to know.

After all, we've walked David's pasture, the pasture of exclusion.

We are weary of society's surface-level system, of being graded according to the inches of our waist, the square footage of our house, the color of our skin, the make of our car, the label of our clothes, the size of our office, the presence of diplomas, the absence of pimples. Don't we weary of such games?

Hard work ignored. Devotion unrewarded. The boss chooses cleavage over character. The teacher picks pet students instead of prepared ones. Parents show off their favorite sons and leave their runts out in the field. Oh, the Goliath of exclusion.

Are you sick of him? Then it's time to quit staring at him. Who cares what he, or they, think? What matters is what your Maker thinks. "The Lord does not see as man sees; for man looks at the outward appearance, but the Lord looks at the heart" (16:7).

Those words were written for the *haqqatons* of society, for misfits and outcasts. God uses them all.

Moses ran from justice, but God used him.

Jonah ran from God, but God used him.

Rahab ran a brothel, Samson ran to the wrong woman, Jacob ran in circles, Elijah ran into the mountains, Sarah ran out of hope, Lot ran with the wrong crowd, but God used them all.

And David? God saw a teenage boy serving him in the backwoods of Bethlehem, at the intersection of boredom and anonymity, and through the voice of a brother, God called, "David! Come in. Someone wants to see you." Human eyes saw a gangly teenager enter the house, smelling like sheep and looking like he needed a bath. Yet, "the Lord said, 'Arise, anoint him; for this is the one!'" (16:12).

God saw what no one else saw: a God-seeking heart. David, for all his foibles, sought God like a lark seeks sunrise. He took after God's heart, because he stayed after God's heart. In the end, that's all God wanted or needed . . . wants or needs. Others measure your waist size or wallet. Not God. He examines hearts. When he finds one set on him, he calls it and claims it.

God examines hearts.
When he finds one set on him, he calls it and claims it.

By the way, remember how I waited for the phone to ring that night? It never did. But the doorbell did.

Long after my hopes were gone and my glove was hung, the doorbell rang. It was the coach. He made it sound as if I were a top choice and he thought an assistant had phoned me. Only later did I learn the truth. I was the last pick. And, save a call from my dad, I might have been left off the team.

But Dad called, and the coach came, and I was glad to play.

The story of young David assures us of this: your Father knows your heart, and because he does, he has a place reserved just for you.

3

RAGING SAULS

S HARON CHECKS her rearview mirror . . . again. She studies the faces of other drivers . . . again. She keeps an eye out for him, because she knows he'll come after her . . . again.

"Nothing will keep me from you" was the message Tony had left on her voice mail. "I'm your husband."

Her ex-husband's paroxysms of anger and flying fists and her black eyes had led to divorce. Still he neglected warnings, ignored restraining orders, and scoffed at the law.

So Sharon checks the rearview mirror . . . again.

Down the road, around the corner, an office worker named Adam does some checking of his own. He peeks in the door of his boss's office, sees the empty chair, and sighs with relief. With any luck, he'll have an hour, maybe two, before the Scrooge of the dot-com world appears in his doorway, likely hungover, angry, and disoriented.

Scrooge Jr. inherited the company from Scrooge Sr. Running the business frustrates Junior. He reroutes his stress toward the employees he needs the most. Such as Adam. Junior rants and raves, gives tongue-lashings daily, and compliments with the frequency of Halley's comet.

Sharon ducks her ex, Adam avoids his boss, and you? What ogres roam your world?

Controlling moms. Coaches from the school of Stalin. The pit-bull math teacher. The self-appointed cubicle commandant. The king who resolves to spear the shepherd boy to the wall.

That last one comes after David. Poor David. The Valley of Elah proved to be boot camp for the king's court. When Goliath lost his head, the Hebrews made David their hero. People threw him a ticker-tape parade and sang, "Saul has slain his thousands, and David his ten thousands" (1 Sam. 18:7).

Saul explodes like the Vesuvius he is. Saul eyes David "from that day forward" (18:9). The king is already a troubled soul, prone to angry eruptions, mad enough to eat bees. David's popularity splashes gasoline on Saul's temper. "I will pin David to the wall!" (18:11).

Saul tries to kill Bethlehem's golden boy six different times. First, he invites David to marry his daughter Michal. Seems like a kind gesture, until you read the crude dowry Saul required. One hundred Philistine foreskins. *Surely one of the Philistines will kill David,* Saul hopes. They don't. David doubles the demand and returns with the proof (18:25–27).

Saul doesn't give up. He orders his servants and Jonathan to kill

David, but they refuse (19:1). He tries with the spear another time but misses (19:10). Saul sends messengers to David's house to kill him, but his wife, Michal, lowers him through a window. David the roadrunner stays a step ahead of Saul the coyote.

Saul's anger puzzles David. What has he done but good? He has brought musical healing to Saul's tortured spirit, hope to the enfeebled nation. He is the Abraham Lincoln of the Hebrew calamity, saving the republic and doing so modestly and honestly. He behaves "wisely in all his ways" (18:14). "All Israel and Judah loved David" (18:16). David behaves "more wisely than all the servants of Saul, so that his name became highly esteemed" (18:30).

Yet, Mount Saul keeps erupting, rewarding David's deeds with flying spears and murder plots. We understand David's question to Jonathan: "What have I done? What is my iniquity, and what is my sin before your father, that he seeks my life?" (20:1).

Jonathan has no answer to give, for no answer exists. Who can justify the rage of a Saul?

Who knows why a father torments a child, a wife belittles her husband, a boss pits employees against each other? But they do. Sauls still rage on our planet. Dictators torture, employers seduce, ministers abuse, priests molest, the strong and mighty control and cajole the vulnerable and innocent. Sauls still stalk Davids.

How does God respond in such cases? Nuke the nemesis? We may want him to. He's been known to extract a few Herods and Pharaohs. How he will treat yours, I can't say. But how he will treat you, I can. He will send you a Jonathan.

God counters Saul's cruelty with Jonathan's loyalty. Jonathan could have been as jealous as Saul. As Saul's son, he stood to inherit the throne. A noble soldier himself, he was fighting Philistines while David was still feeding sheep.

Jonathan had reason to despise David, but he didn't. He was gracious. Gracious because the hand of the Master Weaver took his and David's hearts and stitched a seam between them. "The soul of Jonathan was knit to the soul of David, and Jonathan loved him as his own soul" (18:1).

The hand of the Master Weaver took Jonathan's and David's hearts and stitched a seam between them.

As if the two hearts were two fabrics, God "needle and threaded" them together. So interwoven that when one moved, the other felt it. When one was stretched, the other knew it.

On the very day David defeats Goliath, Jonathan pledges his loyalty.

> Then Jonathan and David made a covenant, because he loved him as his own soul. And Jonathan took off the robe that was on him and gave it to David, with his armor, even to his sword and his bow and his belt. (18:3–4)

Jonathan replaces David's bucolic garment with his own purple robe: the robe of a prince. He presents his own sword to David. He effectively crowns young David. The heir to the throne surrenders his throne.

And, then, he protects David. When Jonathan hears the plots of

Saul, he informs his new friend. When Saul comes after David, Jonathan hides him. He commonly issues warnings like this one: "My father Saul seeks to kill you. Therefore please be on your guard until morning, and stay in a secret place and hide" (19:2).

Jonathan gives David a promise, a wardrobe, and protection. "There is a friend who sticks closer than a brother" (Prov. 18:24). David found such a friend in the son of Saul.

Oh, to have a friend like Jonathan. A soul mate who protects you, who seeks nothing but your interests, wants nothing but your happiness. An ally who lets you be you. You feel safe with that person. No need to weigh thoughts or measure words. You know his or her faithful hand will sift the chaff from the grain, keep what matters, and with a breath of kindness, blow the rest away.[1] God gave David such a friend.

He gave you one as well. David found a companion in a prince of Israel; you can find a friend in the King of Israel, Jesus Christ. Has he not made a covenant with you? Among his final words were these: "I am with you always, even to the end of the age" (Matt. 28:20).

David found a companion in a prince of Israel;
you can find a friend in the King of Israel, Jesus Christ.

Has he not clothed you? He offers you "white garments, that you may be clothed, that the shame of your nakedness may not be revealed" (Rev. 3:18). Christ cloaks you with clothing suitable for heaven.

In fact, he outdoes Jonathan. He not only gives you his robe; he dons your rags. "God made him who had no sin to be sin for us, so that in him we might become the righteousness of God" (2 Cor. 5:21 NIV).

Jesus dresses you. And, like Jonathan, he equips you. You are invited to "put on all of God's armor so that you will be able to stand firm against all strategies and tricks of the Devil" (Eph. 6:11 NLT). From his armory he hands you the belt of truth, the body armor of righteousness, the shield of faith, and the sword of the Spirit, which is the Word of God (vv. 13–17).

Just as Jonathan protected David, Jesus vows to protect you. "I give them eternal life, and they will never perish. No one will snatch them away from me" (John 10:28 NLT).

You long for one true friend? You have one. And because you do, you have a choice. You can focus on your Saul or your Jonathan, ponder the malice of your monster or the kindness of your Christ.

You long for one true friend? You have one.
And because you do, you have a choice. You can . . .
ponder the malice of your monster or
the kindness of your Christ.

Beverly[2] chooses to maximize Christ. Isn't easy. How can you shift your focus away from the man who raped you? He entered Beverly's home under the guise of official business. She had every reason to trust him: personal acquaintance and professional associate. He worked for the state and requested an audience with Beverly. But he took more than her time.

He denied and successfully covered up the deed. As he continues to move up the political ladder, Beverly spots him on the evening news, encounters him at parties. While he feigns innocence, she churns within.

But not like she used to. Two years after the rape she met her Jonathan. A friend told her about Christ—his protection, his provision, and his invitation. She accepted it. Memories of the rape still dog her, but they don't control her. She isn't left alone with her Saul anymore. She seeks Christ rather than revenge; she measures choices against his mercy, not her violator's cruelty. Beverly ponders and praises the living presence of Jesus. Doing so heals her soul.

Major in your evil emperor, if you choose. Paint horns on his picture. Throw darts at her portrait. Make and memorize a list of everything the Spam-brain took: your childhood, career, marriage, health. Live a Saul-saturated life. Wallow in the sludge of pain. You'll feel better, won't you?

Or will you?

Linger too long in the stench of your hurt,
and you'll smell like the toxin you despise.

I spent too much of a high school summer sludging through sludge. Oil field work is dirty enough at best. But the dirtiest job of all? Shoveling silt out of empty oil tanks. The foreman saved such jobs for the summer help. (Thanks, boss.) We donned gas masks, pried open the metal door, and waded into ankle-deep, contaminated mire. My mom burned my work clothes. The stink stuck.

Yours can do the same. Linger too long in the stench of your hurt, and you'll smell like the toxin you despise.

The better option? Hang out with your Jonathan. Bemoan Saul less; worship Christ more. Join with David as he announces:

> The Lord lives!
>> Blessed be my Rock! . . .
>> It is God who avenges me,
>> And subdues the peoples under me;
>> He delivers me from my enemies. . . .
>> You have delivered me from the violent man.
>> Therefore I will give thanks to You, O Lord, among the
> Gentiles,
>> And sing praises to Your name. (Ps. 18:46–49)

Wander freely and daily through the gallery of God's goodness. Catalog his kindnesses. Everything from sunsets to salvation—look at what you have. Your Saul took much, but Christ gave you more! Let Jesus be the friend you need. Talk to him. Spare no detail. Disclose your fear and describe your dread.

Will your Saul disappear? Who knows? And, in a sense, does it matter? You just found a friend for life. What could be better than that?

4

DESPERATE DAYS

THE DESPERATE MAN sits in the corner of the church assembly. Dry mouth, moist palms. He scarcely moves. He feels out of place in a room of disciples, but where else can he go? He just violated every belief he cherishes. Hurt every person he loves. Spent a night doing what he swore he'd never do. And now, on Sunday, he sits and stares. He doesn't speak. *If these people knew what I did....*

Scared, guilty, and alone.

He could be an addict, a thief, a child-beater, a wife-cheater.

He could be a she—single, pregnant, confused. He could be any number of people, for any number of people come to God's people in his condition—hopeless, hapless, helpless.

How will the congregation react? What will he find? Criticism or compassion? Rejection or acceptance? Raised eyebrows or extended hands?

David wonders the same. He's on the lam, a wanted man in Saul's court. His young face decorates post office posters. His name tops Saul's to-kill list. He runs, looking over his shoulder, sleeping with one eye open, and eating with his chair next to the restaurant exit.

What a blurring series of events. Was it just two or three years ago that he was tending flocks in Bethlehem? Back then a big day was watching sheep sleep. Then came Samuel, a ripe-old prophet with a fountain of hair and a horn of oil. As the oil covered David, so did God's Spirit.

David went from serenading sheep to serenading Saul. The overlooked runt of Jesse's litter became the talk of the town, King Arthur to Israel's Camelot years, handsome and humble. Enemies feared him. Jonathan loved him. Michal married him. Saul hated him.

After the sixth attempt on his life, David gets the point. *Saul doesn't like me.* With a price on his head and a posse on his trail, he kisses Michal and life in the court good-bye and runs.

But where can he go? To Bethlehem and jeopardize the lives of his family? Into enemy territory and risk his own? That becomes an option later. For now, he chooses another hideout. He goes to church. "Now David came to Nob, to Ahimelech the priest" (1 Sam. 21:1).

Scholars point to a hill one mile northeast of Jerusalem as the likely site of the ancient city of Nob. There, Ahimelech, the great-grandson of Eli, headed up a monastery of sorts. Eighty-five priests served in Nob, earning it the nickname "the city of the priests" (22:19). David rushes to the small town, seeking sanctuary from his enemies.

His arrival stirs understandable fear in Ahimelech. He "was trembling as he went to meet David" (21:1 GOD'S WORD). What brings a warrior to Nob? What does the son-in-law of the king want?

David buys assurance by lying to the priest:

> The king has ordered me on some business, and said to me, "Do not let anyone know anything about the business on which I send you, or what I have commanded you. . . . Now therefore, what have you on hand? Give me five loaves of bread in my hand, or whatever can be found." (21:2–3)

Desperate, David resorts to mistruth. This surprises us. So far David has been stellar, spotless, stainless—Snow White in a cast of warty-nosed witches. He stayed calm when his brothers snapped; he remained strong when Goliath roared; he kept his cool when Saul lost his.

But now he lies like a mob don at confession. Blatantly. Convincingly. Saul hasn't sent him on a mission. He's not on secret royal business. He's a fugitive. Unfairly, yes. But a fugitive nonetheless. And he lies about it.

The priest does not question David. He has no reason to doubt the skedaddler. He just has no resources with which to help him. The priest has bread, not common bread, but holy bread. The bread of the Presence. Each Sabbath the priest placed twelve loaves of wheat bread on the table as an offering to God. After a week, and only after a week, the priests, and only the priests, could eat the bread. (As if anyone wants week-old bread.) Nonetheless, Ahimelech's options and clerical collar shrink.

David is no priest. And the bread has just been placed on the altar. What's Ahimelech to do? Distribute the bread and violate the law? Keep the bread and ignore David's hunger? The priest looks for a loophole: "There is no common bread on hand; but there is holy bread, if the young men have at least kept themselves from women" (21:4).

Ahimelech wants to know if David and his men have been behaving. Blame it on the smell of fresh bread, but David responds with lie number two and a theological two-step. His men haven't laid eyes, much less hands, on a girl. And the holy bread? He puts an arm around the priest, walks him toward the altar, and suggests, *You know, Ahim, old boy,* "the bread is in effect common, even though it was sanctified in the vessel this day" (21:5). Even holy loaves, David reasons, are still oven baked and wheat based. Bread is bread, right?

David, what are you doing? Is lying not enough? Now you're playing loose with Scripture and putting the soft sell on the preacher?

It works. The priest gives him holy bread, "for there was no bread there but the showbread which had been taken from before the Lord, in order to put hot bread in its place on the day when it was taken away" (21:6).

Ravenous, David gulps down the food. Ahimelech likely gulps as well. He wonders if he has done the right thing. Has he bent the law? Broken the law? Obeyed a higher law? The priest had decided the higher call was a hungry stomach. Rather than dot the *i* of God's code, he met the need of God's child.

And how does David reward Ahimelech's compassion? With another lie! "Is there not here on hand a spear or a sword? For I have brought neither my sword nor my weapons with me, because the king's business required haste" (21:8).

David's faith is wavering. Not too long ago the shepherd's sling was all he needed. Now the one who refused the armor and sword of Saul requests a weapon from the priest. What has happened to our hero?

Simple. He's lost his God-focus. Goliath is on the big screen of David's imagination. As a result, desperation has set in. Lie-spawning, fear-stirring, truth-shading desperation. No place to hide. No food to eat. No recourse. No resource. Teenaged and pregnant, middle-aged and broke, old-aged and sick. . . . Where can the desperate go?

To the spiritually hungry, the church offers nourishment.

They can go to God's sanctuary. God's church. They can look for an Ahimelech, a church leader with a heart for desperate souls.

Ahimelech had given David bread; now David wants a blade. The only weapon in the sanctuary is a relic, the sword of Goliath. The very steel David had used to guillotine the head of the giant. The priests are displaying it like the Accademia Gallery in Florence, Italy, displays Michelangelo's *David*.

"This will do just fine," David says. And the one who entered the sanctuary hungry and weaponless leaves with a bellyful of bread and the sword of a giant.

Author and pastor Eugene Peterson sees this interchange as the function of the church. "A sanctuary," he writes, "is . . . where I, like David, get bread and a sword, strength for the day and weapons for the fight."[1]

To the spiritually hungry, the church offers nourishment:

For I am persuaded that neither death nor life, nor angels nor principalities nor powers, nor things present nor things to come, nor height nor depth, nor any other created thing, shall be able to separate us from the love of God which is in Christ Jesus our Lord. (Rom. 8:38–39)

To the fugitive, the church offers weapons of truth:

And we know that all things work together for good to those who love God, to those who are the called according to His purpose. (Rom. 8:28)

Bread and blades. Food and equipment. The church exists to provide both. Does she succeed in doing so? Not always. People-helping is never a tidy trade, because people who need help don't lead tidy lives. They enter the church as fugitives, seeking shelter from angry Sauls in some cases, bad decisions in others. Ahimelechs of the church (leaders, teachers, pastors, and the like) are forced to choose not between black and white but shades of gray, not between right and wrong but degrees of both.

Pursue the spirit of the law
more than its letter.

Jesus calls the church to lean in the direction of compassion. A millennium later the Son of David remembers the flexibility of Ahimelech.

At that time Jesus went through the grainfields on the Sabbath. And His disciples were hungry, and began to pluck heads of grain and to eat. And when the Pharisees saw it, they said to Him, "Look, Your disciples are doing what is not lawful to do on the Sabbath!" But He said to them, "Have you not read what David did when he was hungry, he and those who were with him: how he entered the house of God and ate the showbread which was not lawful for him to eat, nor for those who were with him, but only for the priests? Or have you not read in the law that on the Sabbath the priests in the temple profane the Sabbath, and are blameless?" (Matt. 12:1–5)

At the end of the sanctuary day, the question is not how many laws were broken but rather, how many desperate Davids were nourished and equipped? Ahimelech teaches the church to pursue the spirit of the law more than its letter.

David teaches the desperate to seek help amidst God's people.

David teaches the desperate to seek help amidst God's people. David stumbles in this story. Desperate souls always do. But at least he stumbles into the right place—into God's sanctuary, where God meets and ministers to hopeless hearts.

For proof, return to the story with which we began: the breathless, disheveled man who sits in the church assembly.

Did I mention the size of the congregation? Small. A dozen or so souls clustered together for strength. Did I tell you the location of the gathering? A borrowed upstairs room in Jerusalem. And the date? Sunday. The Sunday after Friday's crucifixion. The Sunday after Thursday night's betrayal.

A church of desperate disciples.

Peter cowers in the corner and covers his ears, but he can't silence the sound of his empty promise. "I'd *die* for you!" he had vowed (Luke 22:33 MSG). But his courage had melted in the midnight fire and fear. And now he and the other runaways wonder what place God has for them. Jesus answers the question by walking through the door.

---

*God brings bread for our souls ("Peace be with you")
and a sword for the struggle ("Receive the Holy Spirit").*

He brings bread for their souls. "Peace be with you" (John 20:19). He brings a sword for the struggle. "Receive the Holy Spirit" (v. 22).

Bread and swords. He gives both to the desperate.

Still.

5

DRY SEASONS

THE DEAD SEA is dying. Drop by drop, at a rate of three feet a
year, she is shrinking. Galilee sends her fresh fluid through the
Jordanian Canal, water worthy of a Messiah's baptism. But the Dead
Sea impoverishes it: darkening, acidizing, creating a saline cemetery.
You find little life in her waters.

You find little life in her surroundings. Ominous cliffs rise to the
west, flattening out at two thousand feet. Erosion has scarred the
land into a tyranny of caves and ruts and sparse canyons: a home for
hyenas, lizards, buzzards . . . and David. Not by choice, mind you.
He didn't want to swap the palace for the badlands. No one chooses
the wilderness. It comes at you from all directions—heat and rain,
sandstorms and hail. We prefer air-conditioned bedrooms and culs-
de-sac—safety.

But sometimes we have no vote. Calamity hits and the roof rips.

35

The tornado lifts and drops us in the desert. Not the desert in southeastern Israel, but the desert of the soul.

A season of dryness.

Isolation marks such seasons. Saul has effectively and systematically isolated David from every source of stability.

His half-dozen assassination attempts ended David's military career. His pursuit drove a wedge in David's marriage. After David's wife, Michal, helped him escape, Saul demanded an explanation from her. "I had to," she lied. "He threatened to kill me if I didn't help him" (1 Sam. 19:17 TLB). David never trusted his wife again. They stayed married but slept in different beds.

Wilderness begins with disconnections.
It continues with deceit.

David races from Saul's court to Samuel's house. But no sooner does he arrive than someone tells Saul, "Take note, David is at Naioth in Ramah!" (19:19).

David flees to Jonathan, his soul mate. Jonathan wants to help, but what can he do? Leave the court in the hands of a madman? No, Jonathan has to stay with Saul. David can hear the twine popping on the lifeline.

No place in the court.

No position in the army.

No wife, no priest, no friend.

Nothing to do but run. Wilderness begins with disconnections. It continues with deceit.

We saw David's deceit in Nob, the city of the priests. The city was holy; David was anything but. He lied each time he opened his mouth.

David gets worse before he gets better. He escapes to Gath, the hometown of Goliath. He tries to forge a friendship based on a mutual adversary. If your enemy is Saul and my enemy is Saul, we become friends, right?

In this case, wrong.

The Gittites aren't hospitable. "Isn't this David, the king of the land?" they ask. "Isn't he the one the people honor with dances, singing, 'Saul has killed his thousands, and David his ten thousands'?" (21:11 NLT).

David panics. He's a lamb in a pack of wolves. Tall men, taller walls. Piercing glares, piercing spears. We'd like to hear a prayer to his Shepherd; we'd appreciate a pronouncement of God's strength. Don't hold your breath. David doesn't see God. He sees trouble. So he takes matters into his own hands.

He pretends to be insane, scratching on doors and drooling down his beard. Finally the king of Gath says to his men, "'Must you bring me a madman? We already have enough of them around here! Why should I let someone like this be my guest?' So David left Gath and escaped to the cave of Adullam" (21:14–22:1 NLT).

Dare we envision this picture of David? Staring with galvanized eyes. Quivering like jelly. He sticks out his tongue, rolls in the dirt, grunts and grins, spits, shakes, and foams. David feigns something like epilepsy.

The Philistines believed "an epileptic was possessed by Dagon's devil and that he made husbands impotent, women barren, children die, and animals vomit." Fearing that every drop of an epileptic's blood created one more devil, the Philistines drove epileptics out of their towns and into the desert to die.' And that's what they do with David. They shove him out the city gates and leave him with nowhere to go.

He can't go to the court of Saul or the house of Michal, the city of Samuel or the safety of Nob. So he goes to the only place he can—the place where no one goes, because nothing survives. He goes to the desert, the wilderness. To the honeycombed canyons that overlook the Dead Sea. He finds a cave, the cave called Adullam. In it he finds shade, silence, and safety. He stretches on the cool dirt and closes his eyes and begins his decade in the wilderness.

Can you relate to David's story?

Has your Saul cut you off from the position you had and the people you love?

In an effort to land on your feet, have you stretched the truth? Distorted the facts?

Are you seeking refuge in Gath? Under normal circumstances you would never go there. But these aren't normal circumstances, so you loiter in the breeding ground of giants. The hometown of trouble. Her arms or that bar. You walk shady streets and frequent questionable places. And, while there, you go crazy. So the crowd will accept you, so the stress won't kill you, you go wild. You wake up in a Dead Sea cave, in the grottoes of Adullam, at the lowest point of your life, feeling as dumb as a roomful of anvils. You stare out at an arid, harsh, unpeopled future and ask, "What do I do now?"

I suggest you let David be your teacher. Sure, he goes wacko for a few verses. But in the cave of Adullam, he gathers himself. The faithful shepherd boy surfaces again. The giant-killer rediscovers courage. Yes, he has a price on his head. Yes, he has no place to lay his head, but somehow he keeps his head.

He returns his focus to God and finds refuge.

Refuge surfaces as a favorite word of David's. Circle its appearances in the book of Psalms, and you'll count as many as forty-plus appearances in some versions. But never did David use the word more poignantly than in Psalm 57. The introduction to the passage explains its background: "A song of David when he fled from Saul into the cave."

Envision Jesse's son in the dimness: on his knees, perhaps on his face, lost in shadows and thought. He has nowhere to turn. Go home, he endangers his family; to the tabernacle, he imperils the priests. Saul will kill him; Gath won't take him. He lied in the sanctuary and went crazy with the Philistines, and here he sits. All alone.

But then he remembers: he's not. He's not alone. And from the recesses of the cave a sweet voice floats:

Be merciful to me, O God, be merciful to me!
For my soul trusts in You;
And in the shadow of Your wings I will make my refuge. (v. 1)

Make God your refuge. Not your job, your spouse, your reputation, or your retirement account. Make God your refuge. Let him, not Saul, encircle you. Let him be the ceiling that breaks the sunshine, the walls that stop the wind, the foundation on which you stand.

A cave-dweller addressed our church recently. He bore the smell of Adullam. He'd just buried his wife, and his daughter was growing sicker by the day. Yet, in the dry land he found God. I wrote his discovery on the flyleaf of my Bible: "You'll never know that Jesus is all you need until Jesus is all you have."

Wilderness survivors find refuge in God's presence.

They also discover community among God's people.

Soon [David's] brothers and other relatives joined him there. Then others began coming—men who were in trouble or in debt or who were just discontented—until David was the leader of about four hundred men (1 Sam. 22:1–2 NLT).

Not what you'd call a corps of West Point cadets. In trouble, in debt, or discontent. Quite a crew. Misfits, yes. Dregs from the barrel, no doubt. Rejects. Losers. Dropouts.

Just like the church. Are we not the distressed, the debtors, and the discontent?

Take a good look, friends, at who you were when you got called into this life. I don't see many of "the brightest and the best" among you, not many influential, not many from high-society families. Isn't it obvious that God deliberately chose men and women that the culture overlooks and exploits and abuses, chose these "nobodies" to expose the hollow pretensions of the "somebodies"? (1 Cor. 1:26–28 MSG)

Strong congregations are populated with current and former cave dwellers, people who know the terrain of Adullam. They told a few lies in Nob. They went loopy in Gath. And they haven't forgotten it. And because they haven't, they imitate David: they make room for you.

Who is David to turn these men away? He's no candidate for archbishop. He's a magnet for marginal people. So David creates a community of God-seeking misfits. God forges a mighty group out of them: "they came to David day by day to help him, until it was a great army, like the army of God" (1 Chron. 12:22).

Gath. Wilderness. Adullam.

Folly. Loneliness. Restoration.

David found all three. So did Whit Criswell. This Kentucky native was raised in a Christian home. As a young man, he served as an officer in a Christian church. But he fell into gambling, daily risking his income on baseball games. He lost more than he won and found himself in desperate debt to his bookie. He decided to embezzle funds from the bank where he worked. Welcome to Gath.

It was only a matter of time until the auditors detected a problem and called for an appointment. Criswell knew he'd been caught. The night before the examination he couldn't sleep. He resolved to take the path of Judas. Leaving his wife a suicide note, he drove outside of Lexington, parked the car, and put the gun to his head. He couldn't pull the trigger, so he took a practice shot out the car window. He pressed the nose of the barrel back on his forehead and mumbled, "Go ahead and pull the trigger, you no-good slob. This is what you deserve." But he couldn't do it. The fear that he might go to hell kept him from taking his life.

Finally, at dawn, he went home, a broken man. His wife had found the note and called the police. She embraced him. The officers handcuffed him and led him away. He was, at once, humiliated and liberated: humiliated to be arrested in front of family and neighbors, but liberated from the chains of mistruth. He didn't have to lie anymore.

Whit Criswell's Adullam was a prison cell. In it, he came to his senses; he turned back to his faith. Upon release, he plunged into the work of a local church, doing whatever needed to be done.

You'll never know that Jesus is all you need
until Jesus is all you have. Are you in the wilderness?
Find refuge in God's presence. Find comfort in his people.

Over a period of years, he was added to the staff of the congregation. In 1998 another area church asked him to serve as their senior minister. At this writing, that church is one of Kentucky's fastest-growing congregations.[2]

Another David restored.

Are you in the wilderness? Crawl into God the way a fugitive would a cave. Find refuge in God's presence.

Find comfort in his people. Cast your hat in a congregation of folks who are one gift of grace removed from tragedy, addiction, and disaster. Seek community in the church of Adullam.

Refuge in God's presence. Comfort in God's people. Your keys for wilderness survival. Do this, and, who knows, in the midst of this desert you may write your sweetest psalms.

6

GRIEF-GIVERS

T HE MOST SACRED symbol in Oklahoma City, Oklahoma, is a
tree: a sprawling, shade-bearing, eighty-year-old American elm.
Tourists drive from miles around to see her. People pose for pictures
beneath her. Arborists carefully protect her. She adorns posters and
letterhead. Other trees grow larger, fuller, even greener. But not one
is equally cherished. The city treasures the tree, not for her appearance, but her endurance.

She endured the Oklahoma City bombing.

Timothy McVeigh parked his death-laden truck only yards from
her. His malice killed 168 people, wounded 850, destroyed the Alfred
P. Murrah Federal Building, and buried the tree in rubble. No one
expected it to survive. No one, in fact, gave any thought to the dusty,
branch-stripped tree.

But then she began to bud.

Sprouts pressed through damaged bark; green leaves pushed away gray soot. Life resurrected from an acre of death. People noticed. The tree modeled the resilience the victims desired. So they gave the elm a name: the Survivor Tree.[1]

Timothy McVeighs still rock our worlds. They still, inexcusably, inexplicably maim and scar us. We want to imitate the tree—survive the evil, rise above the ruin. But how?

David can give us some ideas. When Saul "McVeighs" his way into David's world, David dashes into the desert, where he finds refuge among the caves near the Dead Sea. Several hundred loyalists follow him. So does Saul. And in two dramatic desert scenes, David models how to give grace to the person who gives nothing but grief.

Scene one. Saul signals for his men to stop. They do. Three thousand soldiers cease their marching as their king dismounts and walks up the mountainside.

The region of En Gedi simmers in the brick-oven heat. Sunrays strike daggerlike on the soldiers' necks. Lizards lie behind rocks. Scorpions linger in the dirt. And snakes, like Saul, seek rest in the cave.

Saul enters the cave "to relieve himself. Now David and his men were hiding far back in the cave" (1 Sam. 24:3 NCV). With eyes dulled from the desert sun, the king fails to notice the silent figures who line the walls.

But don't you know they see him. As Saul heeds nature's call, dozens of eyes widen. Their minds race, and hands reach for daggers. One thrust of the blade will bring Saul's tyranny and their running to an end. But David signals for his men to hold back. He edges along the wall, unsheathes his knife, and cuts not the flesh but the robe of Saul. David then creeps back into the recesses of the cave.

David's men can't believe what their leader has done. Neither can David. Yet his feelings don't reflect theirs. They think he has done too little; he thinks he has done too much. Rather than gloat, he regrets.

> Later David felt guilty because he had cut off a corner of Saul's robe. He said to his men, "May the Lord keep me from doing such a thing to my master! Saul is the Lord's appointed king. I should not do anything against him, because he is the Lord's appointed king!" (24:5–6 NCV)

Saul exits the cave, and David soon follows. He lifts the garment corner and, in so many words, shouts, "I could have killed you, but I didn't."

Saul looks up, stunned, and wonders aloud, "If a man finds his enemy, will he let him get away safely?" (24:19).

David will. More than once.

Just a couple of chapters later, Saul, once again, is hunting David. David, once again, out-shrewds Saul. While the camp of the king sleeps, daredevil David and a soldier stealth their way through the ranks until they stand directly over the snoring body of the king. The soldier begs, "This is the moment! God has put your enemy in your grasp. Let me nail him to the ground with his spear. One hit will do it, believe me; I won't need a second!" (26:8 MSG).

But David will not have it. Rather than take Saul's life, he takes Saul's spear and water jug and sneaks out of the camp. From a safe distance he awakens Saul and the soldiers with an announcement: "GOD put your life in my hands today, but I wasn't willing to lift a finger against God's anointed" (26:23 MSG).

Once again, David spares Saul's life.

Once again, David displays the God-saturated mind. Who dominates his thoughts? "May the LORD . . . the LORD delivered . . . the LORD's anointed . . . in the eyes of the LORD" (26:23–24).

Once again, we think about the purveyors of pain in our own lives. It's one thing to give grace to friends, but to give grace to those who give us grief? Could you? Given a few uninterrupted moments with the Darth Vader of your days, could you imitate David?

Perhaps you could. Some people seem graced with mercy glands. They secrete forgiveness, never harboring grudges or reciting their hurts. Others of us (most of us?) find it hard to forgive our Sauls.

Vengeance fixes your attention at life's ugliest moments.

We forgive the one-time offenders, mind you. We dismiss the parking-place takers, date-breakers, and even the purse snatchers. We can move past the misdemeanors, but the felonies? The repeat offenders? The Sauls who take our youth, retirement, or health?

Were that scoundrel to seek shade in your cave or lie sleeping at your feet . . . would you do what David did? Could you forgive the scum who hurt you?

Failure to do so could be fatal. "Resentment kills a fool, and envy slays the simple" (Job 5:2 NIV).

Vengeance fixes your attention at life's ugliest moments. Score-settling freezes your stare at cruel events in your past. Is this where you want to look? Will rehearsing and reliving your hurts make you a better person? By no means. It will destroy you.

I'm thinking of an old comedy routine. Joe complains to Jerry about the irritating habit of a mutual friend. The guy pokes his finger in Joe's chest as he talks. It drives Joe crazy. So he resolves to get even. He shows Jerry a small bottle of highly explosive nitroglycerin tied to a string. He explains, "I'm going to wear this around my neck, letting the bottle hang over the exact spot where I keep getting poked. Next time he sticks his finger in my chest, he'll pay for it."

Not nearly as much as Joe will, right? Enemy destroyers need two graves. "It is foolish to harbor a grudge" (Eccles. 7:9 TEV). An eye for an eye becomes a neck for a neck and a job for a job and a reputation for a reputation. When does it stop? It stops when one person imitates David's God-dominated mind.

Enemy destroyers need two graves.

He faced Saul the way he faced Goliath—by facing God more so. When the soldiers in the cave urged David to kill Saul, look who occupied David's thoughts: "The LORD forbid that I should do this thing to my master, the Lord's anointed, to stretch out my hand against him, seeing he is the anointed of the Lord" (1 Sam. 24:6).

When David called out to Saul from the mouth of the cave, "David stooped with his face to the earth, and bowed down" (24:8).

Then he reiterated his conviction: "I will not stretch out my hand against my lord, for he is the Lord's anointed" (24:10).

In the second scene, during the nighttime campsite attack, David maintained his belief: "Who can stretch out his hand against the Lord's anointed, and be guiltless?" (26:9).

In these two scenes I count six times when David called Saul "the Lord's anointed." Can you think of another term David might have used? *Buzzkill* and *epoxy brain* come to my mind. But not to David's. He saw, not Saul the enemy, but Saul the anointed. He refused to see his grief-giver as anything less than a child of God. David didn't applaud Saul's behavior; he just acknowledged Saul's proprietor— God. David filtered his view of Saul through the grid of heaven. The king still belonged to God, and that gave David hope.

Some years ago a rottweiler attacked our golden retriever puppy at a kennel. The worthless animal climbed out of its run and into Molly's and nearly killed her. He left her with dozens of gashes and a dangling ear. My feelings toward that mutt were less than Davidic. Leave the two of us in a cave, and only one would have exited. I wrote a letter to the dog's owner, urging him to put the dog to sleep.

But when I showed the letter to the kennel owner, she begged me to reconsider. "What that dog did was horrible, but I'm still training him. I'm not finished with him yet."

God would say the same about the rottweiler who attacked you. "What he did was unthinkable, unacceptable, inexcusable, but I'm not finished yet."

Your enemies still figure into God's plan. Their pulse is proof: God hasn't given up on them. They may be out of God's will, but not out of his reach. You honor God when you see them, not as his failures, but as his projects.

Besides, who assigned us the task of vengeance? David understood this. From the mouth of the cave, he declared, "May the LORD decide between you and me. May the LORD take revenge on you for what you did to me. However, I will not lay a hand on you.... the LORD must be the judge. He will decide" (24:12, 15 GOD'S WORD).

See your enemies, not as God's failures,
but as God's projects.

God occupies the only seat on the supreme court of heaven. He wears the robe and refuses to share the gavel. For this reason Paul wrote, "Don't insist on getting even; that's not for you to do. 'I'll do the judging,' says God. 'I'll take care of it'" (Rom. 12:19 MSG).

Revenge removes God from the equation. Vigilantes displace and replace God. "I'm not sure you can handle this one, Lord. You may punish too little or too slowly. I'll take this matter into my hands, thank you."

Is this what you want to say? Jesus didn't. No one had a clearer sense of right and wrong than the perfect Son of God. Yet, "when he suffered, he didn't make any threats but left everything to the one who judges fairly" (1 Pet. 2:23 GOD'S WORD).

Only God assesses accurate judgments. We impose punishments too slight or severe. God dispenses perfect justice. Vengeance is his job. Leave your enemies in God's hands. You're not endorsing their misbehavior when you do. You can hate what someone did without letting hatred consume you. Forgiveness is not excusing.

Nor is forgiveness pretending. David didn't gloss over or sidestep Saul's sin. He addressed it directly. He didn't avoid the issue, but he did avoid Saul. "Saul returned home, but David and his men went up to the stronghold" (1 Sam. 24:22 NIV).

Do the same. Give grace, but, if need be, keep your distance. You can forgive the abusive husband without living with him. Be quick to give mercy to the immoral pastor, but be slow to give him a pulpit. Society can dispense grace and prison terms at the same time. Offer the child molester a second chance, but keep him off the playgrounds.

Forgiveness is not foolishness.

Forgiveness is, at its core, choosing to see your offender with different eyes. When some Moravian missionaries took the message of God to the Eskimos, the missionaries struggled to find a word in the native language for forgiveness. They finally landed on this cumbersome twenty-four-letter choice: *issumagijoujungnainermik*. This formidable assembly of letters is literally translated "not being able to think about it anymore."[2]

Forgiveness . . . is choosing to see your offender with different eyes.

To forgive is to move on, not to think about the offense anymore. You don't excuse him, endorse her, or embrace them. You just route thoughts about them through heaven. You see your enemy as God's child and revenge as God's job.

By the way, how can we grace-recipients do anything less? Dare we ask God for grace when we refuse to give it? This is a huge issue in Scripture. Jesus was tough on sinners who refused to forgive other sinners. Remember his story about the servant freshly forgiven a debt of millions who refused to forgive a debt equal to a few dollars? He stirred the wrath of God: "You evil servant! I forgave you that tremendous debt. . . . Shouldn't you have mercy . . . just as I had mercy on you?" (Matt. 18:32–33 NLT).

In the final sum, we give grace because we've been given grace. We survive because we imitate the Survivor Tree. We reach our roots beyond the bomb zone. We tap into moisture beyond the explosion. We dig deeper and deeper until we draw moisture from the mercy of God.

We, like Saul, have been given grace.

We, like David, can freely give it.

7

BARBARIC BEHAVIOR

E RNEST GORDON groans in the Death House of Chungkai, Burma. He listens to the moans of the dying and smells the stench of the dead. Pitiless jungle heat bakes his skin and parches his throat. Had he the strength, he could wrap one hand around his bony thigh. But he has neither the energy nor the interest. Diphtheria has drained both; he can't walk; he can't even feel his body. He shares a cot with flies and bedbugs and awaits a lonely death in a Japanese prisoner-of-war camp.

How harsh the war has been on him. He entered World War II in his early twenties, a robust Highlander in Scotland's Argyle and Sutherland Brigade. But then came the capture by the Japanese, months of backbreaking labor in the jungle, daily beatings, and slow starvation. Scotland seems forever away. Civility, even farther.

The Allied soldiers behave like barbarians, stealing from each other, robbing dying colleagues, fighting for food scraps. Servers shortchange rations so they can have extra for themselves. The law of the jungle has become the law of the camp.

Gordon is happy to bid it adieu. Death by disease trumps life in Chungkai. But then something wonderful happens. Two new prisoners, in whom hope still stirs, are transferred to the camp. Though also sick and frail, they heed a higher code. They share their meager meals and volunteer for extra work. They cleanse Gordon's ulcerated sores and massage his atrophied legs. They give him his first bath in six weeks. His strength slowly returns and, with it, his dignity.

Their goodness proves contagious, and Gordon contracts a case. He begins to treat the sick and share his rations. He even gives away his few belongings. Other soldiers do likewise. Over time, the tone of the camp softens and brightens. Sacrifice replaces selfishness. Soldiers hold worship services and Bible studies.

Twenty years later, when Gordon served as chaplain of Princeton University, he described the transformation with these words:

> Death was still with us—no doubt about that. But we were slowly being freed from its destructive grip. . . . Selfishness, hatred . . . and pride were all anti-life. Love . . . self-sacrifice . . . and faith, on the other hand, were the essence of life . . . gifts of God to men. . . . Death no longer had the last word at Chungkai.[1]

Selfishness, hatred, and pride—you don't have to go to a POW camp to find them. A dormitory will do just fine. As will the boardroom of a corporation or the bedroom of a marriage or the backwoods of a county. The code of the jungle is alive and well. *Every man for himself. Get all you can, and can all you get. Survival of the fittest.*

Does the code contaminate your world? Do personal possessive pronouns dominate the language of your circle? *My* career, *my* dreams, *my* stuff. I want things to go *my* way on *my* schedule. If so, you know how savage this giant can be. Yet, every so often, a diamond glitters in the mud. A comrade shares, a soldier cares, or Abigail, stunning Abigail, stands on your trail.

She lived in the days of David and was married to Nabal, whose name means "fool" in Hebrew. He lived up to the definition.

Think of him as the Saddam Hussein of the territory. He owned cattle and sheep and took pride in both. He kept his liquor cabinet full, his date life hot, and motored around in a stretch limo. His NBA seats were front row, his jet was Lear, and he was prone to hop over to Vegas for a weekend of Texas Hold 'em. Half a dozen linebacker-size security guards followed him wherever he went.

Nabal needed the protection. He was "churlish and ill-behaved— a real Calebbite dog. . . . He is so ill-natured that one cannot speak to him" (1 Sam. 25:3, 17)[2] He learned people skills in the local zoo. He never met a person he couldn't anger or a relationship he couldn't spoil. Nabal's world revolved around one person—Nabal. He owed nothing to anybody and laughed at the thought of sharing with anyone.

Especially David.

David played a Robin Hood role in the wilderness. He and his six hundred soldiers protected the farmers and shepherds from brigands and Bedouins. Israel had no highway patrol or police force, so David and his mighty men met a definite need in the countryside. They

guarded with enough effectiveness to prompt one of Nabal's shepherds to say, "Night and day they were a wall around us all the time
we were herding our sheep near them" (25:16 NIV).

David and Nabal cohabited the territory with the harmony of
two bulls in the same pasture. Both strong and strong-headed. It was
just a matter of time before they collided.

Trouble began to brew after the harvest. With sheep sheared and
hay gathered, it was time to bake bread, roast lamb, and pour wine.
Take a break from the furrows and flocks and enjoy the fruit of the
labor. As we pick up the story, Nabal's men are doing just that.

David hears of the gala and thinks his men deserve an invitation.
After all, they've protected the man's crops and sheep, patrolled the
hills and secured the valleys. They deserve a bit of the bounty. David
sends ten men to Nabal with this request: "We come at a happy
time, so be kind to my young men. Please give anything you can find
for them and for your son David" (25:8 NCV).

Boorish Nabal scoffs at the thought:

Who is David, and who is the son of Jesse? There are many servants nowadays who break away each one from his master. Shall
I then take my bread and my water and my meat that I have
killed for my shearers, and give it to men when I do not know
where they are from? (25:10–11)

Nabal pretends he's never heard of David, lumping him in with
runaway slaves and vagabonds. Such insolence infuriates the messengers, and they turn on their heels and hurry back to David with
a full report.

David doesn't need to hear the news twice. He tells the men to form a posse. Or, more precisely, "Strap on your swords!" (25:12 MSG)

Four hundred men mount up and take off. Eyes glare. Nostrils flare. Lips snarl. Testosterone flows. David and his troops thunder down on Nabal, the scoundrel, who obliviously drinks beer and eats barbecue with his buddies. The road rumbles as David grumbles, "May God do his worst to me if Nabal and every cur in his misbegotten brood isn't dead meat by morning!" (25:22 MSG).

Hang on. It's the Wild West in the Ancient East.

Olive branches do more good than battle-axes ever will.

Then, all of a sudden, beauty appears. A daisy lifts her head in the desert; a swan lands at the meat packing plant; a whiff of perfume floats through the men's locker room. Abigail, the wife of Nabal, stands on the trail. Whereas he is brutish and mean, she is "intelligent and good-looking" (25:3 MSG).

Brains *and* beauty. Abigail puts both to work. When she learns of Nabal's crude response, she springs into action. With no word to her husband, she gathers gifts and races to intercept David. As David and his men descend a ravine, she takes her position, armed with "two hundred loaves of bread, two skins of wine, five sheep dressed out and ready for cooking, a bushel of roasted grain, a hundred raisin cakes, and two hundred fig cakes, . . . all loaded on some donkeys" (25:18 MSG).

Four hundred men rein in their rides. Some gape at the food; others gawk at the female. She's good lookin' with good cookin', a combination that stops any army. (Picture a neck-snapping blonde showing up at boot camp with a truck full of burgers and ice cream.)

Abigail's no fool. She knows the importance of the moment. She stands as the final barrier between her family and sure death. Falling at David's feet, she issues a plea worthy of a paragraph in Scripture. "On me, my lord, on me let this iniquity be! And please let your maidservant speak in your ears, and hear the words of your maidservant" (25:24).

She doesn't defend Nabal but agrees that he is a scoundrel. She begs not for justice but forgiveness, accepting blame when she deserves none. "Please forgive the trespass of your maidservant" (25:28). She offers the gifts from her house and urges David to leave Nabal to God and avoid the dead weight of remorse.

Her words fall on David like July sun on ice. He melts.

Blessed be God, the God of Israel. He sent you to meet me! . . . A close call! . . . if you had not come as quickly as you did, stopping me in my tracks, by morning there would have been nothing left of Nabal but dead meat. . . . I've heard what you've said and I'll do what you've asked. (25:32–35 MSG)

David returns to camp. Abigail returns to Nabal. She finds him too drunk for conversation so waits until the next morning to describe how close David came to camp and Nabal came to death. "Right then and there he had a heart attack and fell into a coma. About ten days later GOD finished him off and he died" (25:37–38 MSG).

When David learns of Nabal's death and Abigail's sudden availability, he thanks God for the first and takes advantage of the second.

Unable to shake the memory of the pretty woman in the middle of the road, he proposes, and she accepts. David gets a new wife, Abigail a new home, and we have a great principle: beauty can overcome barbarism.

Meekness saved the day that day. Abigail's gentleness reversed a river of anger. Humility has such power. Apologies can disarm arguments. Contrition can defuse rage. Olive branches do more good than battle-axes ever will. "Soft speech can crush strong opposition" (Prov. 25:15 NLT).

Abigail teaches so much. The contagious power of kindness. The strength of a gentle heart. Her greatest lesson, however, is to take our eyes from her beauty and set them on someone else's. She lifts our thoughts from a rural trail to a Jerusalem cross. Abigail never knew Jesus. She lived a thousand years before his sacrifice. Nevertheless, her story prefigures his life.

"Soft speech can crush strong opposition"
(Prov. 25:15 NLT).

Abigail placed herself between David and Nabal. Jesus placed himself between God and us. Abigail volunteered to be punished for Nabal's sins. Jesus allowed heaven to punish him for yours and mine. Abigail turned away the anger of David. Didn't Christ shield you from God's?

He was our "Mediator who can reconcile God and people. He is the man Christ Jesus. He gave his life to purchase freedom for everyone" (1 Tim. 2:5–6 NLT). Who is a mediator but one who stands in between? And what did Christ do but stand in between God's anger and our punishment? Christ intercepted the wrath of heaven.

Something remotely similar happened at the Chungkai camp. One evening after work detail, a Japanese guard announced that a shovel was missing. The officer kept the Allies in formation, insisting that someone had stolen it. Screaming in broken English, he demanded that the guilty man step forward. He shouldered his rifle, ready to kill one prisoner at a time until a confession was made.

Christ lived the life we could not live and took the punishment we could not take to offer the hope we cannot resist.

A Scottish soldier broke ranks, stood stiffly at attention, and said, "I did it." The officer unleashed his anger and beat the man to death. When the guard was finally exhausted, the prisoners picked up the man's body and their tools and returned to camp. Only then were the shovels recounted. The Japanese soldier had made a mistake. No shovel was missing after all.[3]

Who does that? What kind of person would take the blame for something he didn't do?

When you find the adjective, attach it to Jesus. "God has piled all our sins, everything we've done wrong, on him, on him" (Isa. 53:6 MSG). God treated his innocent Son like the guilty human race, his Holy One like a lying scoundrel, his Abigail like a Nabal.

Christ lived the life we could not live and took the punishment we could not take to offer the hope we cannot resist. His sacrifice begs us to ask this question: if he so loved us, can we not love each other? Having been forgiven, can we not forgive? Having feasted at the table of grace, can we not share a few crumbs? "My dear, dear friends, if God loved us like this, we certainly ought to love each other" (1 John 4:11 MSG).

Do you find your Nabal world hard to stomach? Then do what David did: stop staring at Nabal. Shift your gaze to Christ. Look more at the Mediator and less at the troublemakers. "Don't let evil get the best of you; get the best of evil by doing good" (Rom. 12:21 MSG). One prisoner can change a camp. One Abigail can save a family. Be the beauty amidst your beasts and see what happens.

8

SLUMP GUNS

GOLIATH OWNS a slump gun: a custom-designed, twelve zillion meter, .338 magnum with a fluted barrel and a heart-seeking scope. It fires, not bullets, but sadness. It takes, not lives, but smiles. It inflicts, not flesh wounds, but faith wounds.

Ever been hit?

If you can't find your rhythm, you have. If you can't seem to get to first base (or out of bed), you have. Every step forward gets lost in two steps backward.

Relationships sour.

Skies darken and billow.

Your nights defy the sunrise.

You've been slumped.

Problems are the Sioux. You are Custer. You feel like you're on your last stand.

David feels like it is his. Saul has been getting the best of David, leaving him sleeping in caves, lurking behind trees. Six hundred soldiers depend on David for leadership and provision. These six hundred men have wives and children. David has two wives of his own (all but guaranteeing tension in his tent).

Running from a crazed king. Hiding in hills. Leading a ragtag group of soldiers. Feeding more than a thousand mouths.

The slump gun finds its mark. Listen to David: "One of these days I will be destroyed by the hand of Saul. The best thing I can do is to escape to the land of the Philistines. Then Saul will give up searching for me anywhere in Israel, and I will slip out of his hand" (1 Sam. 27:1 NIV).

No hope and, most of all, no God. David focuses on Saul. He hangs Saul's poster on his wall and replays his voice messages. David immerses himself in his fear until his fear takes over: "I will be destroyed."

He knows better. In brighter seasons and healthier moments, David modeled heaven's therapy for tough days. The first time he faced the Philistines in the wilderness, "David inquired of the Lord" (23:2). When he felt small against his enemy, "David inquired of the Lord" (23:4). When attacked by the Amalekites, "David inquired of the Lord" (30:8). Puzzled about what to do after the death of Saul, "David inquired of the Lord" (2 Sam. 2:1). When crowned as king and pursued by the Philistines, "David inquired of the Lord" (5:19). David defeated them, yet they mounted another attack, so "David inquired of the Lord" (5:23). David kept God's number on speed dial.

Confused? David talked to God. Challenged? He talked to God. Afraid? He talked to God . . . most of the time. But not this time. On this occasion, David talks to himself. He doesn't even seek the counsel of his advisers. When Saul first lashed out, David turned to Samuel. As the attacks continued, David asked Jonathan for advice. When weaponless and breadless, he took refuge among the priests of Nob. In this case, however, David consults David.

Poor choice. Look at the advice he gives himself: "Now I will perish one day by the hand of Saul" (1 Sam. 27:1 NASB).

No you won't, David. Don't you remember the golden oil of Samuel on your face? God has anointed you. Don't you remember God's promise through Jonathan? "You shall be king over Israel" (23:17). Have you forgotten the assurance God gave you through Abigail? "The LORD will keep all his promises of good things for you. He will make you leader over Israel" (25:30 NCV). God has even assured your safety through Saul. "I know indeed that you shall surely be king" (24:20).

But in the wave of weariness, David hits the pause button on good thoughts and thinks:

> Sooner or later, Saul's going to get me. The best thing I can do
> is escape to Philistine country. Saul will count me a lost cause
> and quit hunting me down in every nook and cranny of Israel.
> I'll be out of his reach for good. (27:1 MSG)

So David leaves, and Saul calls off the hunt. David defects into the hands of the enemy. He leads his men into the land of idols and false gods and pitches his tent in Goliath's backyard. He plops down in the pasture of Satan himself.

Initially, David feels relief. Saul gives up the chase. David's men can sleep with both eyes closed. Children can attend kindergarten, and wives can unpack the suitcases. Hiding out with the enemy brings temporary relief.

Doesn't it always?

Stop resisting alcohol, and you'll laugh—for a while.

Move out on your spouse, and you'll relax—for a time.

Indulge in the porn, and you'll be entertained—for a season.

But then talons of temptation sink in. Waves of guilt crash in. The loneliness of breaking up rushes in. "There's a way of life that looks harmless enough; look again—it leads straight to hell. Sure, those people appear to be having a good time, but all that laughter will end in heartbreak" (Prov. 14:12–13 MSG).

Hiding out with the enemy brings only temporary relief.

That "amen" you just heard came from David on high. He can tell you. Listen to the third stanza of his song of the slump. In verse one, "he wore out." So, "he got out." And in order to survive in the enemy camp, David sells out.

He strikes a deal with Achish, the king of Gath: "Give me a place in one of the cities in the country, that I may live there; for why should *your servant* live in the royal city with you?" (1 Sam. 27:5 NASB, emphasis mine).

Note David's self-assigned title: the "servant" of the enemy king. The once-proud son of Israel and conqueror of Goliath lifts a toast to the foe of his family.

Achish welcomes the deal. He grants David a village, Ziklag, and asks only that David turn against his own people and kill them. As far as Achish knows, David does. But David actually raids the enemies of the Hebrews:

> Now David and his men went up and raided the Geshurites, the Girzites and the Amalekites.... Whenever David attacked an area, he did not leave a man or woman alive, but took sheep and cattle, donkeys and camels, and clothes. Then he returned to Achish. (27:8–9 NIV)

Not David's finest hour. He lies to the Philistine king and covers up his deceit with bloodshed. He continues this duplicity for sixteen months. From this season no psalms exist. His harp hangs silent. The slump mutes the minstrel.

Things get worse before they get better.

The Philistines decide to attack King Saul. David and his men opt to switch sides and join the opposition. Envision U.S. Marines joining the Nazis. They journey three days to the battlefield, get rejected, and travel three days home. "The Philistine officers said, ... 'He's not going into battle with us. He'd switch sides in the middle of the fight!'" (29:4 MSG).

David leads his unwanted men back to Ziklag, only to find the village burned to the ground. The Amalekites had destroyed it and kidnapped all the wives, sons, and daughters. When David and his men see the devastation, they weep and weep until they are "exhausted with weeping" (30:4 MSG).

Rejected by the Philistines. Pillaged by the Amalekites. No country to fight for. No family to come home to. Can matters grow worse? They can. Venom flares in the soldiers' eyes. David's men start looking for rocks. "The people in their bitterness said he should be stoned" (30:6 God's Word).

We have to wonder, is David regretting his decision? Longing for simpler days in the wilderness? The good ol' cave days? No Philistine rejection or Amalekite attacks there. His men loved him. His wives were with him.

Now, in the ruins of Ziklag with men selecting stones to throw at him, does he regret his prayerless choice to get out and sell out?

Slumps: the petri dish for bad decisions, the incubator for wrong turns, the assembly line of regretful moves. How we handle our tough times stays with us for a long time.

How we handle our tough times stays with us for a long time.

How do you handle yours? When hope takes the last train and joy is nothing but the name of the girl down the street . . . when you are tired of trying, tired of forgiving, tired of hard weeks or hard-headed people . . . how do you manage your dark days?

With a bottle of pills or scotch? With an hour at the bar, a day at the spa, or a week at the coast? Many opt for such treatments. So many, in fact, that we assume they reenergize the sad life. But do they? No one denies that they help for a while, but over the long haul? They numb the pain, but do they remove it?

Or are we like the sheep on the Turkish cliff? Who knows why the first one jumped over the edge. Even more bizarre are the fifteen hundred others who followed, each leaping off the same overhang.

The first 450 animals died. The thousand that followed survived only because the pile of corpses cushioned their fall.[1]

We, like sheep, follow each other over the edge, falling headlong into bars and binges and beds. Like David, we crash into Gath, only to find that Gath has no solution.

Is there a solution? Indeed there is. Doing right what David did wrong.

He failed to pray. Do the opposite: *be quick to pray*. Stop talking to yourself. Talk to Christ, who invites. "Are you tired? Worn out? Burned out on religion? Come to me. Get away with me and you'll recover your life. I'll show you how to take a real rest" (Matt. 11:28 MSG).

God, who is never downcast, never tires of your down days.

David neglected good advice. Learn from his mistake. Next time you lack the will to go on, *seek healthy counsel*.

You won't want to. Slumping people love slumping people. Hurting people hang with hurting people. We love those who commiserate and avoid those who correct. Yet correction and direction are what we need.

I discovered the importance of healthy counsel in a half-Ironman triathlon. After the 1.2 mile swim and the 56-mile bike ride, I didn't have much energy left for the 13.1 mile run. Neither did the fellow jogging next to me. I asked him how he was doing and soon regretted posing the question.

"This stinks. This race is the dumbest decision I've ever made." He had more complaints than a taxpayer at the IRS. My response to him? "Good-bye." I knew if I listened too long, I'd start agreeing with him.

I caught up with a sixty-six-year-old grandmother. Her tone was just the opposite. "You'll finish this," she encouraged. "It's hot, but at least it's not raining. One step at a time. . . . Don't forget to hydrate. . . . Stay in there." I ran next to her until my heart was lifted and my legs were aching. I finally had to slow down. "No problem," she said, waving as she kept going.

Which of the two describes the counsel you seek? "Refuse good advice and watch your plans fail; take good counsel and watch them succeed" (Prov. 15:22 MSG).

Be quick to pray, seek healthy counsel, and don't give up.

---

*Be quick to pray, seek healthy counsel,
and don't give up.*

Don't make the mistake of Florence Chadwick. In 1952 she attempted to swim the chilly ocean waters between Catalina Island and the California shore. She swam through foggy weather and choppy seas for fifteen hours. Her muscles began to cramp, and her resolve weakened. She begged to be taken out of the water, but her mother, riding in a boat alongside, urged her not to give up. She kept trying but grew exhausted and stopped swimming. Aids lifted her out of the water and into the boat. They paddled a few more minutes, the mist broke, and she discovered that the shore was less than a half mile away. "All I could see was the fog," she explained at a news conference. "I think if I could have seen the shore, I would have made it."[2]

Take a long look at the shore that awaits you. Don't be fooled by the fog of the slump. The finish may be only strokes away. God may be, at this moment, lifting his hand to signal Gabriel to grab the trumpet. Angels may be assembling, saints gathering, demons trembling. Stay at it! Stay in the water. Stay in the race. Stay in the fight. Give grace, one more time. Be generous, one more time. Teach one more class, encourage one more soul, swim one more stroke.

Take a long look at the shore that awaits you.
Don't be fooled by the fog of the slump.
The finish may be only strokes away.

David did. Right there in the smoldering ruins of Ziklag, he found strength. After sixteen months in Gath. After the Philistine rejection, the Amalekite attack, and the insurrection by his men, he remembered what to do. "David found strength in the Lord his God" (1 Sam. 30:6 NIV).

It's good to have you back, David. We missed you while you were away.

9

PLOPPING POINTS

I RECENTLY SAW a woman walking a dog on a leash. Change that. I saw a woman *pulling* a dog *with* a leash. The day was hot, brutally. The dog had stopped, totally. He'd plopped, belly down, in wet grass, swapping blistering pavement for a cool lawn.

The woman tugged and tugged. She'd have had more success pulling a parked semi.

The dog's get-up-and-go had got up and gone, so down he went.

He's not the last to do so. Have you ever reached your "plopping point"?

Blame it on your boss. "We need you to take *one more* case."

Your spouse. "I'll be out late *one more* night this week."

Your parents. "I have *one more* chore for you to do."

Your friend. "I need just *one more* favor."

The problem? You've handled, tolerated, done, forgiven, and taken until you don't have one more "one more" in you. You are one tired puppy. So down you plop. *Who cares what the neighbors think. Who cares what the Master thinks. Let them yank the leash all they want; I ain't taking one more step.*

But unlike the dog, you don't plop in the grass. If you are like David's men, you plop down at Brook Besor.

Don't feel bad if you've never heard of the place. Most haven't, but more need to. The Brook Besor narrative deserves shelf space in the library of the worn-out. It speaks tender words to the tired heart.

The story emerges from the ruins of Ziklag. David and his six hundred soldiers return from the Philistine war front to find utter devastation. A raiding band of Amalekites had swept down on the village, looted it, and taken the women and children hostage. The sorrow of the men mutates into anger, not against the Amalekites, but against David. After all, hadn't he led them into battle? Hadn't he left the women and children unprotected? Isn't he to blame? Then he needs to die. So they start grabbing stones.

What else is new? David is growing accustomed to such treatment. His family ignored him. Saul raged against him. And now David's army, which, if you remember, sought him out, not vice versa, has turned against him. David is a psycho in the making, rejected by every significant circle in his life. This could be his worst hour.

But he makes it one of his best.

While six hundred men stoke their anger, David seeks his God. "But David strengthened himself in the Lord his God" (1 Sam. 30:6).

How essential that we learn to do the same. Support systems

don't always support. Friends aren't always friendly. Pastors can wander off base and churches get out of touch. When no one can help, we have to do what David does here. He turns toward God.

"Shall I go after these raiders? Can I catch them?"

"Go after them! Yes, you'll catch them! Yes, you'll make the rescue!" (30:8 MSG).

(I used to believe only saints could talk with God like this. I'm beginning to think God will talk with anyone in such a fashion and saints are the ones who take him up on his offer.)

Freshly commissioned, David redirects the men's anger toward the enemy. They set out in pursuit of the Amalekites. Keep the men's weariness in mind. They still bear the trail dust of a long campaign and haven't entirely extinguished their anger at David. They don't know the Amalekites' hideout, and, if not for the sake of their loved ones, they might give up.

Indeed, two hundred do. The army reaches a brook called Besor, and they dismount. Soldiers wade in the creek and splash water on their faces, sink tired toes in cool mud, and stretch out on the grass. Hearing the command to move on, two hundred choose to rest. "You go on without us," they say.

How tired does a person have to be to abandon the hunt for his own family?

The church has its quorum of such folks. Good people. Godly people. Only hours or years ago they marched with deep resolve. But now fatigue consumes them. They're exhausted. So beat-up and worn down that they can't summon the strength to save their own flesh and blood. Old age has sucked their oxygen. Or maybe it was a deflating string of defeats. Divorce can leave you at the brook.

Addiction can as well. Whatever the reason, the church has its share of people who just sit and rest.

And the church must decide. What do we do with the Brook Besor people? Berate them? Shame them? Give them a rest but measure the minutes? Or do we do what David did? David let them stay.

The church must decide.
What do we do with the Brook Besor people?

He and the remaining four hundred fighters resume the chase. They plunge deeper and deeper, growing more discouraged with each passing sand dune. The Amalekites have a large lead and have left no clues. But then David hits the jackpot. "They found an Egyptian in the field, and brought him to David; and they gave him bread and he ate, and they let him drink water" (30:11).

The Egyptian is a disabled servant who weighs more than he is worth, so the Amalekites left him to starve in the desert. David's men nurse him back to life with figs and raisins and ask the servant to lead them to the campsite of his old cronies. He is happy to oblige.

David and his men swoop down upon the enemy like hawks on rats. Every Israelite woman and child is rescued. Every Amalekite either bites the dust or hits the trail, leaving precious plunder behind. David goes from scapegoat to hero, and the whooping and hollering begin.

The punch line, however, is yet to be read. To feel the full force of it, imagine the thoughts of some of the players in this story.

The rescued wives. You've just been snatched from your home and dragged through the desert. You've feared for your life and clutched your kids. Then, one great day, the good guys raid the camp. Strong arms sweep you up and set you in front of a camel hump. You thank God for the SWAT team who snatched you and begin searching the soldiers' faces for your husband.

"Honey!" you yell. "Honey! Where are you?"

Your rescuer reins the camel to a halt. "Uh," he begins, "uh . . . your honey stayed at the camp."

"He did what?"

"He hung with the guys at Brook Besor."

I don't know if Hebrew women had rolling pins, but if they did, they might begin slapping them about this moment. "Besor, eh? I'll tell you who'll be sore."

The rescue squad. When David called, you risked your life. Now, victory in hand, you gallop back to Brook Besor. You crest the ridge overlooking the camp and see the two hundred men below.

"You leeches."

While you fought, they slept. You went to battle; they went to matinees and massage therapists. They shot eighteen holes and stayed up late playing poker.

You might feel the way some of David's men felt: "Because they did not go with us, we will not give them any of the spoil that we have recovered, except for every man's wife and children" (30:22).

Rescued wives: angry.

Rescuers: resentful.

And what about the two hundred men who had rested? Worms have higher self-esteem. They feel as manly as a lace doily.

A Molotov cocktail of emotions is stirred, lit, and handed to David. Here's how he defuses it:

> Don't do that after what the Lord has given us. He has protect-
> ed us and given us the enemy who attacked us. Who will listen
> to what you say? The share will be the same for the one who
> stayed with the supplies as for the one who went into battle. All
> will share alike. (30:23–24 NCV)

Note David's words: they "stayed with the supplies," as if this had been their job. They hadn't asked to guard supplies; they wanted to rest. But David dignifies their decision to stay.

David did many mighty deeds in his life. He did many foolish deeds in his life. But perhaps the noblest was this rarely discussed deed: he honored the tired soldiers at Brook Besor.

It's okay to rest.
Jesus fights when you cannot.

Someday somebody will read what David did and name their church the Congregation at Brook Besor. Isn't that what the church is intended to be? A place for soldiers to recover their strength?

In his great book about David, *Leap Over a Wall*, Eugene Peterson tells of a friend who sometimes signs her letters "Yours at the Brook Besor."[1] I wonder how many could do the same. Too tired to fight. Too ashamed to complain. While others claim victories, the weary sit in silence. How many sit at the Brook Besor?

If you are listed among them, here is what you need to know: it's okay to rest. Jesus is your David. He fights when you cannot. He goes where you cannot. He's not angry if you sit. Did he not invite, "Come off by yourselves; let's take a break and get a little rest" (Mark 6:31 MSG)?

Are you weary? Catch your breath. Are you strong?
Reserve passing judgment on the tired.

Brook Besor blesses rest.

Brook Besor also cautions against arrogance. David knew the victory was a gift. Let's remember the same. Salvation comes like the Egyptian in the desert, a delightful surprise on the path. Unearned. Undeserved. Who are the strong to criticize the tired?

Are you weary? Catch your breath. We need your strength.

Are you strong? Reserve passing judgment on the tired. Odds are, you'll need to plop down yourself. And when you do, Brook Besor is a good story to know.

10

UNSPEAKABLE GRIEF

You might hear the news from a policeman: "I'm sorry. He didn't survive the accident."

You might return a friend's call, only to be told, "The surgeon brought bad news."

Too many spouses have heard these words from grim-faced soldiers: "We regret to inform you . . ."

In such moments, spring becomes winter, blue turns to gray, birds go silent, and the chill of sorrow settles in. It's cold in the valley of the shadow of death.

David's messenger isn't a policeman, friend, or soldier. He is a breathless Amalekite with torn clothing and hair full of dirt who stumbles into Camp Ziklag with the news: "The people have fled from the battle, many of the people are fallen and dead, and Saul and Jonathan his son are dead also" (2 Sam. 1:4).

David knows the Hebrews are fighting the Philistines. He knows Saul and Jonathan are in for the battle of their lives. He's been awaiting the outcome. When the messenger presents David with Saul's crown and bracelet, David has undeniable proof—Saul and Jonathan are dead.

Jonathan. Closer than a brother. He had saved David's life and sworn to protect his children.

Saul. God's chosen. God's anointed. Yes, he had hounded David. He had badgered David. But he was still God's anointed.

God's chosen king—dead.

David's best friend—dead.

Leaving David to face yet another giant—the giant of grief.

We've felt his heavy hand on our shoulders. Not in Ziklag, but in emergency rooms, in children's hospitals, at car wrecks, and on battlefields. And we, like David, have two choices: flee or face the giant.

We, like David, have two choices:
flee or face the giant.

Many opt to flee grief. Captain Woodrow Call urged young Newt to do so. In the movie *Lonesome Dove*, Call and Newt are part of an 1880s Texas-to-Montana cattle drive. When a swimming swarm of water moccasins end the life of Newt's best friend, Call offers bereavement counsel, western style. At the burial, in the shade of elms and the presence of cowboys, he advises, "Walk away from it, son. That's the only way to handle death. Walk away from it."

What else can you do? The grave stirs such unspeakable hurt and unanswerable questions, we're tempted to turn and walk. Change the subject, avoid the issue. Work hard. Drink harder. Stay busy. Stay distant. Head north to Montana and don't look back.

Yet we pay a high price when we do. Bereavement comes from the word *reave*. Look up *reave* in the dictionary, and you'll read "to take away by force, plunder, rob." Death robs you. The grave plunders moments and memories not yet shared: birthdays, vacations, lazy walks, talks over tea. You are bereaved because you've been robbed.

Normal is no more and never will be again. After the wife of C. S. Lewis died of cancer, he wrote, "Her absence is like the sky, spread over everything."[1]

Just when you think the beast of grief is gone, you hear a song she loved or smell the cologne he wore or pass a restaurant where the two of you used to eat. The giant keeps showing up.

And the giant of grief keeps stirring up. Stirring up . . .

Anxiety. "Am I next?"

Guilt. "Why did I tell him . . ." "Why didn't I say to her . . ."

Wistfulness. You see intact couples and long for your mate. You see parents with kids and yearn for your child.

The giant stirs up insomnia, loss of appetite, forgetfulness, thoughts of suicide. Grief is not a mental illness, but it sure feels like one sometimes.

Captain Call didn't understand this.

Your friends may not understand this.

You may not understand this. But please try. Understand the gravity of your loss. You didn't lose at Monopoly or misplace your keys. You can't walk away from this. At some point, within minutes or months, you need to do what David did. Face your grief.

Upon hearing of the deaths of Saul and Jonathan, "David lamented" (2 Sam. 1:17). The warrior wept. The commander buried a bearded face in callous hands and cried. He "ripped his clothes to ribbons. All the men with him did the same. They wept and fasted the rest of the day, grieving the death of Saul and his son Jonathan, and also the army of God and the nation Israel, victims in a failed battle" (1:11–12 MSG).

Wailing warriors covered the hills, a herd of men walking, moaning, weeping, and mourning. They tore clothing, pounded the ground, and exhaled hurt.

You need to do the same. Flush the hurt out of your heart, and when the hurt returns, flush it again. Go ahead, cry a Mississippi.

Jesus did. Next to the tomb of his dear friend, "Jesus wept" (John 11:35). Why would he do such a thing? Does he not know of Lazarus's impending resurrection? He's one declaration from seeing his friend exit the grave. He'll see Lazarus before dinner. Why the tears?

Death amputates a limb of your life.

Amid the answers we think we know and the many we don't is this one: death stinks.

Death amputates a limb of your life. So Jesus wept. And in his tears we find permission to shed our own. F. B. Meyer wrote:

Jesus wept. Peter wept. The Ephesian converts wept on the neck of the Apostle whose face they were never to see again. Christ stands by each mourner, saying, "Weep, my child; weep, for I have wept."

Tears relieve the burning brain, as a shower in the electric clouds. Tears discharge the insupportable agony of the heart, as an overflow lessens the pressure of the flood against the dam. Tears are the material out of which heaven weaves its brightest rainbow.[2]

We don't know how long Jesus wept. We don't know how long David wept. But we know how long we weep, and the time seems so truncated. Egyptians dress in black for six months. Some Muslims wear mourning clothes for a year. Orthodox Jews offer prayers for a deceased parent every day for eleven months. Just fifty years ago rural Americans wore black armbands for a period of several weeks.[3] And today? Am I the only one who senses that we hurry our hurts?

Tears are the material out of which heaven weaves its brightest rainbow. —F. B. Meyer

---

Grief takes time. Give yourself some. "Sages invest themselves in hurt and grieving" (Eccles. 7:4 MSG). *Lament* may be a foreign verb in our world but not in Scripture's. Seventy percent of the psalms are poems of sorrow. Why, the Old Testament includes a book of lamentations. The son of David wrote, "Sorrow is better than laughter, for sadness has a refining influence on us" (Eccles. 7:3 NLT).

We spelunk life's deepest issues in the cave of sorrow. Why am I here? Where am I headed? Cemetery strolls stir hard yet vital questions. David indulged the full force of his remorse: "I am worn out from sobbing. Every night tears drench my bed; my pillow is wet from weeping" (Ps. 6:6 NLT).

We spelunk life's deepest issues in the cave of sorrow.
Why am I here? Where am I headed?

And then later: "I am dying from grief; my years are shortened by sadness. Misery has drained my strength; I am wasting away from within" (Ps. 31:10 NLT).

Are you angry with God? Tell him. Disgusted with God? Let him know. Weary of telling people you feel fine when you don't? Tell the truth. My friends Thomas and Andrea Davidson did. A stray bullet snatched their fourteen-year-old son, Tyler, out of their lives. Tom writes:

We were bombarded by the question, "How are you doing?" . . . What I really wanted to tell everyone was, "How do you think we are doing? Our son is dead, our life is miserable, and I wish the world would end."[4]

David might have used different language. Then again, maybe not. One thing for sure, he refused to ignore his grief.

The mighty warriors—fallen, fallen!

Women of Israel, weep for Saul. . . .
O my dear brother Jonathan,
I'm crushed by your death.
Your friendship was a miracle-wonder,
love far exceeding anything I've known—
or ever hope to know.

The mighty warriors—fallen, fallen. (2 Sam. 1:19, 24,
26–27 MSG)

David wept as creatively as he worshiped, and—underline this—
"David sang this lament over Saul and his son Jonathan, and gave
orders that everyone in Judah learn it by heart" (1:17–18 MSG).

David called the nation to mourning. He rendered weeping a
public policy. He refused to gloss over or soft-pedal death. He faced
it, fought it, challenged it. But he didn't deny it. As his son Solomon
explained, "There is . . . a time to mourn" (Eccles. 3:1, 4 NIV).

Give yourself some. Face your grief with tears, time, and—one
more—face your grief with truth. Paul urged the Thessalonians to
grieve, but he didn't want the Christians to "carry on over them like
people who have nothing to look forward to, as if the grave were the
last word" (1 Thess. 4:13 MSG).

God has the last word on death. And, if you listen, he will tell
you the truth about your loved ones. They've been dismissed from
the hospital called Earth. You and I still roam the halls, smell the
medicines, and eat green beans and Jell-O off plastic trays. They,
meanwhile, enjoy picnics, inhale springtime, and run through knee-
high flowers. You miss them like crazy, but can you deny the truth?

They have no pain, doubt, or struggle. They really are happier in heaven.

And won't you see them soon? Life blisters by at mach speed. "You have made my days a mere handbreadth; the span of my years is as nothing before you. Each man's life is but a breath" (Ps. 39:5 NIV).

He knows the sorrow of a grave. He buried his son. But he also knows the joy of resurrection. And, by his power, you will too.

When you drop your kids off at school, do you weep as though you'll never see them again? When you drop your spouse at the store and park the car, do you bid a final forever farewell? No. When you say, "I'll see you soon," you mean it. When you stand in the cemetery and stare down at the soft, freshly turned earth and promise, *I'll see you soon*, you speak truth. Reunion is a splinter of an eternal moment away.

There is no need for you to "to grieve like the rest of men, who have no hope" (1 Thess. 4:13 NIV).

So go ahead, face your grief. Give yourself time. Permit yourself tears. God understands. He knows the sorrow of a grave. He buried his son. But he also knows the joy of resurrection. And, by his power, you will too.

11

BLIND INTERSECTIONS

I CAN GET LOST anywhere. Seriously. Anywhere. The simplest map confuses me; the clearest trail bewilders me. I couldn't track an elephant through four feet of snow. I can misread instructions to the bathroom down the hall. Indeed, once I did and embarrassed several women in a fast-food restaurant in Fort Worth.

My list of mishaps reads like comedy ideas for the Pink Panther.

- I once got lost in my hotel. I told the receptionist my key wasn't working, only to realize I'd been on the wrong floor trying to open the wrong door.
- Several years ago I was convinced my car had been stolen from the airport parking garage. It hadn't; I was in the wrong garage.

- I once boarded the wrong flight and awoke in the wrong city.
- While driving from Houston to San Antonio, I exited the freeway to gas up. I reentered the freeway and drove for thirty minutes before I realized I was heading back to Houston.
- While in Seattle, I left my hotel room in plenty of time for my speaking engagement, but when I saw highway signs advertising the Canadian border, I knew I'd be late.
- I once went for a morning jog, returned to the hotel, and ate. I'd eaten two portions of the free buffet before I remembered my hotel had no breakfast bar. I was in the wrong place.

If geese had my sense of direction, they'd spend winters in Alaska. I can relate to Columbus, who, as they say, didn't know where he was going when he left, didn't know where he was when he got there, and didn't know where he had been when he got back.

Can you relate? Of course you can. We've all scratched our heads a time or two, if not at highway intersections, at least at the crossroads of life. The best of navigators have wondered, do I . . .

- take the job or leave it?
- accept the marriage proposal or pass?
- leave home or remain home?
- build or buy?

One of life's giant-size questions is *How can I know what God wants me to do?* and David asks it. He's just learned of the deaths of Saul and

Jonathan. Suddenly the throne is empty, and David's options are open. But before he steps out, he looks up:

> It happened after this that David inquired of the LORD, saying, "Shall I go up to any of the cities of Judah?" And the LORD said to him, "Go up." David said, "Where shall I go up?" And He said, "To Hebron." (2 Sam. 2:1)

David makes a habit of running his options past God. And he does so with a fascinating tool. The ephod. Trace its appearance to David's initial escape from Saul. David seeks comfort from the priests of Nob. Saul accuses the priests of harboring the fugitive, and, consistent with Saul's paranoia, he murders them. One priest by the name of Abiathar, however, flees. He escapes with more than just his life; he escapes with the ephod.

> After Abiathar took refuge with David, he joined David in the raid on Keilah, bringing the Ephod with him.
>
> . . . David got wind of Saul's strategy to destroy him and said to Abiathar the priest, "Get the Ephod." Then David prayed to God: "God of Israel, I've just heard that Saul plans to come to Keilah and destroy the city because of me. Will the city fathers of Keilah turn me over to him? Will Saul come down and do what I've heard? O God, God of Israel, tell me!"
>
> GOD replied, "He's coming down."
>
> "And will the head men of Keilah turn me and my men over to Saul?"

And GOD said, "They'll turn you over."

So David and his men got out of there. (1 Sam. 23:6, 9–13 MSG)

David dons the ephod, speaks to God, and receives an answer. Something similar occurs after the destruction of Ziklag. With his village in ruins and his men enraged,

> he ordered Abiathar the priest, son of Ahimelech, "Bring me the Ephod so I can consult God." Abiathar brought it to David.
>
> Then David prayed to GOD, "Shall I go after these raiders? Can I catch them?"
>
> The answer came, "Go after them! Yes, you'll catch them! Yes, you'll make the rescue!" (30:7–8 MSG)

What is happening? What is this ephod? What made it so effective? And are they sold in department stores?

The ephod originated in the era of the wilderness wanderings. Moses presented the first one to Aaron, the priest. It was an ornate vest, woven of white linen, in-wrought with threads of blue, purple, scarlet, and gold. A breastplate bearing twelve precious stones adorned the vest. The breastplate contained one or two, maybe three, resplendent diamonds or diamondlike stones. These stones had the names Urim and Thummim. No one knows the exact meaning of the terms, but "light" and "perfection" lead the list.

God revealed his will to the priests through these stones. How? Ancient writers have suggested several methods. The stones

- illuminated when God said yes;

- contained moving letters that gathered to form a response;
- were sacred lots that, upon being cast, would reveal an answer.[1]

While we speculate on the technique, we don't need to guess at the value. Would you not cherish such a tool? When faced with a puzzling choice, David could, with reverent heart, make a request, and God would answer.

Will Saul come after me? He will.

Will the men capture me? They will.

Should I pursue the enemy? You should.

Will I overtake them? You will.

The God who guided David guides you.

Oh, that God would do the same for us. That we could ask and he would answer. That we could cry out and he would reply. Wouldn't you love to have an ephod? Who's to say you don't? God hasn't changed. He still promises to guide us:

The LORD says, "I will guide you along the best pathway for your life. I will advise you and watch over you." (Ps. 32:8 NLT)

Seek his will in all you do, and he will direct your paths. (Prov. 3:6 NLT)

Whether you turn to the right or to the left, your ears will hear a voice behind you, saying, "This is the way; walk in it." (Isa. 30:21 NIV)

My sheep recognize my voice; I know them, and they follow me. (John 10:27 NLT)

The God who guided David guides you. You simply need to consult your Maker. I wish I'd sought counsel before I made a recent decision. I awoke early one morning for a meeting. When searching for some breakfast, I spotted a plastic bag of cookies in the kitchen. Denalyn and our daughter Sara had just attended a school bake sale, so I thought, *What great luck! Breakfast cookies. Denalyn must have set them out for me.*

I ate one and found it very chewy, almost gummy. *Interesting texture,* I thought. *Reminds me of pita bread.* I ate a second. The taste was a bit subtle for my preference, but when mixed with coffee, it made for an interesting option. I grabbed a third for the road. I would have grabbed the fourth, but only one remained, so I left it for Denalyn.

Later in the day she phoned. "Looks like someone has been in the bag."

"It was me," I admitted. "I've had better breakfast cookies, but those weren't bad."

"Those weren't breakfast cookies, Max."

"They weren't?"

"No."

"What were they?"

"Homemade dog biscuits."

"Oh . . ." That explained a lot. That explained the gummy texture and the tasteless taste. That also explained why all day each time I scratched my belly, my leg kicked. (Not to mention my sudden interest in fire hydrants.)

You have a Bible? Read it.

I should've consulted the maker. We need to consult ours.

Maybe you have no Urim and Thummim stones, but . . .

You have a Bible? Read it.

Has any other book ever been described in this fashion: "For the word of God is living and active. Sharper than any double-edged sword, it penetrates even to dividing soul and spirit, joints and marrow; it judges the thoughts and attitudes of the heart" (Heb. 4:12 NIV)?

"Living and active." The words of the Bible have life! Nouns with pulse rates. Muscular adjectives. Verbs darting back and forth across the page. God works though these words. The Bible is to God what a surgical glove is to the surgeon. He reaches through them to touch deep within you.

Haven't you felt his touch?

In a late, lonely hour, you read the words "I will never fail you. I will never forsake you" (Heb. 13:5 NLT). The sentences comfort like a hand on your shoulder.

When anxiety termites away at your peace, someone shares this passage: "Do not be anxious about anything, but in everything, by prayer and petition, with thanksgiving, present your requests to God" (Phil. 4:6 NIV). The words stir a sigh from your soul.

Or perhaps laziness is knocking on your door. You're considering a halfhearted effort when Colossians 3:23 comes to mind: "Whatever you do, work at it with all your heart, as working for the Lord, not for men" (NIV). Such words can cut, can't they?

Put them to use. "Let the words of Christ, in all their richness, live in your hearts and make you wise. Use his words to teach and counsel each other" (Col. 3:16 NLT).

Don't make a decision, whether large or small, without sitting before God with open Bible, open heart, open ears, imitating the prayer of Samuel: "Your servant is listening" (1 Sam. 3:10 NLT).

You have a Bible? Read it.

You have a family of faith? Consult it.

Others have asked your question. You aren't the first to face your problem. Others have stood where you stand and wondered what you wonder. Seek their advice. "Consider the outcome of their way of life, and imitate their faith" (Heb. 13:7 NRSV).

You have a family of faith? Consult it.

Is your marriage tough? Find a strong one. Wrestling with business ethics? Seek sage advice from a Christian businessperson. Battling midlife decisions? Before you abandon your family and cash in your retirement, take time to get counsel. "The way of a fool seems right to him, but a wise man listens to advice" (Prov. 12:15 NIV).

You don't need an ephod to wear or stones to consult; you have God's family. He will speak to you through it. And he will speak to you through your own conscience.

You have a heart for God? Heed it.

Christ nudges the Christ-possessed heart. "God is working in you to help you want to do and be able to do what pleases him" (Phil. 2:13 NCV). What does your heart tell you to do? What choice spawns the greatest sense of peace?

Christ nudges the Christ-possessed heart.

Some years ago Denalyn and I were a signature away from moving from one house to another. The structure was nice, and the price was fair. . . . It seemed a wise move. But I didn't feel peaceful about it. The project stirred unease and restlessness. I finally drove to the builder's office and removed my name from his list. To this day I can't pinpoint the source of the discomfort. I just didn't feel peaceful about it.

A few months ago I was asked to speak at a racial unity conference. I intended to decline but couldn't bring myself to do so. The event kept surfacing in my mind like a cork in a lake. Finally I agreed. Returning from the event, I still couldn't explain the impression to be there. But I felt peaceful about the decision, and that was enough.

Sometimes a choice just "feels" right. When Luke justified the writing of his gospel to Theophilus, he said, "Since I myself have carefully investigated everything from the beginning, it seemed good also to me to write an orderly account for you, most excellent Theophilus" (1:3 NIV).

Did you note the phrase "it seemed good also to me"? These

words reflect a person standing at the crossroads. Luke pondered his options and selected the path that "seemed good."

Jude did likewise. He intended to dedicate his epistle to the topic of salvation, but he felt uneasy with the choice. Look at the third verse of his letter.

Dear friends, I wanted very much to write you about the salvation we all share. But I felt the need to write you about something else: I want to encourage you to fight hard for the faith that was given the holy people of God once and for all time. (NCV)

Again the language. "I wanted . . . But I felt . . ." From whence came Jude's feelings? Did they not come from God? The same God who "is working in you to help you want to do . . . what pleases him" (Phil. 2:13 NCV).

God creates the "want to" within us.

God will not lead you to violate his Word.

Be careful with this. People have been known to justify stupidity based on a "feeling." "I felt God leading me to cheat on my wife . . . disregard my bills . . . lie to my boss . . . flirt with my married neighbor." Mark it down: God will not lead you to violate his Word. He will not contradict his teaching. Be careful with the phrase "God led me . . ." Don't banter it about. Don't disguise your sin as a leading of God. He will not lead you to lie, cheat, or hurt. He will faithfully lead you through the words of his Scripture and the advice of his faithful.

You need no ephod or precious stones; you have a heart in which God's Spirit dwells. As F. B. Meyer wrote a century ago:

> Each child of God has his own Urim and Thummim stone, . . . a conscience void of offense, a heart cleansed in the blood of Christ, a spiritual nature which is pervaded and filled by the Holy Spirit of God. . . . Are you in difficulty about your way? Go to God with your question; get direction from the light of his smile or the cloud of his refusal. . . . get alone, where the lights and shadows of earth cannot interfere, where the disturbance of self-will does not intrude, where human opinions fail to reach— . . . wait there silent and expectant, though all around you insist on immediate decision or action—the will of God will be made clear; and you will have . . . a new conception of God, [and] a deeper insight into his nature.[2]

You have a heart for God? Heed it.

A family of faith? Consult it.

A Bible? Read it.

You have all you need to face the giant-size questions of your life. Most of all you have a God who loves you too much to let you wander. Trust him . . . and avoid the dog biscuits.

12

STRONGHOLDS

P ETE SITS on the street and leans his head against a building. He'd like to beat his head against it. He just messed up again. Everyone misspeaks occasionally. Pete does so daily. He blurts wrong words like a whale spouts salt water, spraying folly everywhere. He always hurts someone, but tonight he hurt his dear friend. Oh, Pete and his quick-triggered tongue.

Then there's Joe and his failures. The poor guy can't hold a job. His career rivals the Rocky Mountains—up, down; cold, hot; lush, barren. He tried his hand at the family business. They fired him. Tried his skills as a manager. Got canned and jailed. Now he sits in prison, future as bleak as the Mojave Desert. No one could fault him for feeling insecure; he's flopped at each opportunity.

So has she—not at work but at marriage. Her first one failed. So did her second. By the collapse of the third, she knew the names of the court clerk's grandkids. If her fourth trip to divorce court didn't convince her, the fifth removed all doubt. She is destined for marital flops.

People and their proverbial hang-ups. Pete always speaks before he thinks. Joe always fails where he should succeed. This dear woman wins at marriage as often as a burro wins at Churchill Downs.

And you. Does one prevailing problem leech your life?

Some are prone to cheat. Others quick to doubt. Maybe you worry. Yes, everyone worries some, but you own the national distributorship of anxiety. Perhaps you are judgmental. Sure, everybody can be critical, but you pass more judgments than a federal judge.

What is that one weakness, bad habit, rotten attitude? Where does Satan have a stronghold within you? Ahh, there is the fitting word—*stronghold:* a fortress, citadel, thick walls, tall gates. It's as if the devil staked a claim on one weakness and constructed a rampart around it. "You ain't touching this flaw," he defies heaven, placing himself squarely between God's help and your

- explosive temper,
- fragile self-image,
- freezer-size appetite,
- distrust for authority.

Seasons come and go, and this Loch Ness monster still lurks in the water-bottom of your soul. He won't go away. He lives up to both sides of his compound name: *strong* enough to grip like a vise and stubborn enough to *hold* on. He clamps like a bear trap—the harder you shake, the more it hurts.

Strongholds: old, difficult, discouraging challenges.

That's what David faced when he looked at Jerusalem. When you and I think of the city, we envision temples and prophets. We picture Jesus teaching, a New Testament church growing. We imagine a thriving, hub-of-history capital.

When David sees Jerusalem in 1000 BC, he sees something else. He sees a millennium-old, cheerless fortress, squatting defiantly on the spine of a ridge of hills. A rugged outcropping elevates her. Tall walls protect her. Jebusites indwell her. No one bothers them. Philistines fight the Amalekites. Amalekites fight the Hebrews. But the Jebusites? They are a coiled rattlesnake in the desert. Everyone leaves them alone.

Everyone, that is, except David. The just-crowned king of Israel has his eye on Jerusalem. He's inherited a divided kingdom. The people need, not just a strong leader, but strong headquarters. David's present base of Hebron sits too far south to enlist the loyalties of the northern tribes. But if he moves north, he'll isolate the south. He seeks a neutral, centralized city.

He wants Jerusalem. We can only wonder how many times he's stared at her walls. He grew up in Bethlehem, only a day's walk to the south. He hid in the caves in the region of En Gedi, not far south. Surely he noticed Jerusalem. Somewhere he pegged the place as the perfect capital. The crown had scarcely been resized for his head when he set his eyes on his newest Goliath.

And the king and his men went to Jerusalem against the
Jebusites, the inhabitants of the land, who spoke to David, saying,
"You shall not come in here; but the blind and the lame will repel
you," . . . Nevertheless David took the stronghold of Zion (that
is, the City of David). Now David said on that day, "Whoever
climbs up by way of the water shaft and defeats the Jebusites . . .
he shall be chief and captain." . . . Then David dwelt in the
stronghold, and called it the City of David. (2 Sam. 5:6–9)

This regrettably brief story tantalizes us with the twofold appearance of the term *stronghold*. In verse 7, "David took the stronghold,"
and in verse 9, "David dwelt in the stronghold."

Jerusalem meets the qualifications of one: an old, difficult, and
discouraging fortress. From atop the turrets, Jebusite soldiers have
ample time to direct arrows at any would-be wall climbers. And discouraging? Just listen to the way the city-dwellers taunt David.
"You'll never get in here. . . . Even the blind and lame could keep
you out!" (5:6 NLT).

The Jebusites pour scorn on David like Satan dumps buckets of
discouragement on you:

- "You'll never overcome your bad habits."
- "Born white trash; gonna die white trash."
- "Think you can overcome your addiction? Think again."

If you've heard the mocking David heard, your story needs the
word David's has. Did you see it? Most hurry past it. Let's not. Pull
out a pen and underline this twelve-letter masterpiece.

Nevertheless.

"Nevertheless David took the stronghold . . ."

Granted, the city was old. The walls were difficult. The voices were discouraging . . . *Nevertheless* David took the stronghold.

Wouldn't you love God to write a *nevertheless* in your biography? Born to alcoholics, *nevertheless* she led a sober life. Never went to college, *nevertheless* he mastered a trade. Didn't read the Bible until retirement age, *nevertheless* he came to a deep and abiding faith.

Wouldn't you love God to write a nevertheless *in your biography?*

We all need a *nevertheless*. And God has plenty to go around. Strongholds mean nothing to him. Remember Paul's words? "We use God's mighty weapons, not mere worldly weapons, to knock down the Devil's strongholds" (2 Cor. 10:4 NLT).

You and I fight with toothpicks; God comes with battering rams and cannons. What he did for David, he can do for us. The question is, will we do what David did? The king models much here.

David turns a deaf ear to old voices. Those mockers strutting on the wall tops? David ignores them. He dismisses their words and goes about his work.

Nehemiah, on these same walls, took an identical approach. In his case, however, he was atop the stones, and the mockers stood at the base. Fast-forward five hundred years from David's time, and you will see that the bulwarks of Jerusalem are in ruins, and many of her people are in captivity. Nehemiah heads up a building program to restore the fortifications. Critics tell him to stop. They plan to interfere with his work. They list all the reasons the stones can't and shouldn't be restacked. But Nehemiah won't listen to them. "I am doing a great work, so that I cannot come down. Why should the work cease while I leave it and go down to you?" (Neh. 6:3). Nehemiah knew how to press the mute button on his dissenters.

Jesus did too. He responded to Satan's temptations with three terse sentences and three Bible verses. He didn't dialogue with the devil. When Peter told Christ to sidestep the cross, Jesus wouldn't entertain the thought. "Get behind Me, Satan!" (Matt. 16:23). A crowd of people ridiculed what he said about a young girl: "'The girl is not dead, only asleep.' But the people laughed at him" (Matt. 9:24 NCV). You know what Jesus did with the naysayers? He silenced them. "After the crowd had been thrown out of the house, Jesus went into the girl's room and took hold of her hand, and she stood up" (9:25 NCV).

David, Nehemiah, and Jesus practiced selective listening. Can't we do the same?

Two types of thoughts continually vie for your attention. . . .
One proclaims God's strengths; the other lists your failures.

Two types of thoughts continually vie for your attention. One says, "Yes you can." The other says, "No you can't." One says, "God will help you." The other lies, "God has left you." One speaks the language of heaven; the other deceives in the vernacular of the Jebusites. One proclaims God's strengths; the other lists your failures. One longs to build you up; the other seeks to tear you down.

And here's the great news: you select the voice you hear. Why listen to the mockers? Why heed their voices? Why give ear to pea-brains and scoffers when you can, with the same ear, listen to the voice of God?

Why listen to the mockers . . . when you can, with the same ear, listen to the voice of God?

Do what David did. Turn a deaf ear to old voices. And, as you do, open your eyes to new choices. When everyone else saw walls, David saw tunnels. Others focused on the obvious. David searched for the unusual. Since he did what no one expected, he achieved what no one imagined. Get creative with your problem solving.

I know a young couple who battled the stronghold of sexual temptation. They wanted to save sex for the honeymoon but didn't know if they could. So they did what David did. They tried a different approach. They enlisted the support of an understanding married couple. They put the older couple's phone number on speed dial and asked their permission to call them, regardless of the hour, when the temptation was severe. The wall was tall, so they took the tunnel.

I had a friend who battled the stronghold of alcohol. He tried a fresh tactic. He gave me and a few others permission to slug him in the nose if we ever saw him drinking. The wall was too tall, so he tried the tunnel.

One woman counters her anxiety by memorizing long sections of Scripture. A traveling sales rep asks hotels to remove the television from his room so he won't be tempted to watch adult movies. Another man grew so weary of his prejudice that he moved into a minority neighborhood, made new friends, and changed his attitude.

If the wall is too tall, try a tunnel.

David found fresh hope in a hole outside the Jerusalem walls. So can you. Not far from David's tunnel lies the purported tomb of Christ. What David's tunnel did for him, the tomb of Jesus can do for you. "God's power is very great for us who believe. That power is the same as the great strength God used to raise Christ from the dead and put him at his right side in the heavenly world" (Eph. 1:19–20 NCV).

Do what David did.

Turn a deaf ear to the old voices.

Open a wide eye to the new choices.

Who knows, you may be a prayer away from a *nevertheless*. God loves to give them.

He gave one to Pete. Remember him? Speak-now-and-think-later Pete? God released Satan's stronghold on his tongue. For proof, read Peter's Pentecost sermon in Acts 2. God turned impetuous Peter into the apostle Peter (Luke 22:54–62).

And Joe, the failure? Fired by his family. Jailed by his employer . . . Can Jobless Joe ever amount to anything? Joseph did. He became prime minister of Egypt (Gen. 37–50).

What about the five-time divorcée? The woman whom men discarded, Jesus discipled. Last report had her introducing her entire village to Christ. The Samaritan woman was Jesus's first missionary (John 4:1–42). Further proof that "God's mighty weapons . . . knock down the Devil's strongholds" (2 Cor. 10:4 NLT).

Peter stuck his foot in his mouth.

Joseph was imprisoned in Egypt.

The Samaritan woman had been married five times.

Jesus was dead in the grave . . .

Nevertheless, Peter preached, Joseph ruled, the woman shared, Jesus rose—and you?

You fill in the blank. Your *nevertheless* awaits you.

13

Distant Deity

ONE MAN DEAD and one man dancing. One flat on the ground, the other leaping in the air. The dead man is Uzzah the priest. The dancing man is David the king. Readers of 2 Samuel don't know what to do with either.

A little background will help.

The death of the first and the dancing of the second had something do with the ark of the covenant, a rectangular box commissioned by Moses. The chest was not large: three feet, nine inches tall and two feet, three inches wide. A trio of the most precious Hebrew artifacts indwelt the ark: a gold jar of unspoiled manna, Aaron's walking stick that had budded long after it was cut, and the precious stone tablets that had felt the engraving finger of God. A heavy golden plate, called the mercy seat, served as a lid to the chest. Two cherubim of gold, with outstretched wings, faced each other and looked down on the golden lid. They represented the majesty of Jehovah watching over the law and the needs of the people. The ark symbolized God's provision (the manna), God's power (the staff), God's precepts (the commandments), and, most of all, God's presence.

During the temple era, the high priest would be granted a once-a-year audience with the ark. After offering personal sacrifices of repentance, he would enter the holy of holies with, according to legend, a rope tied to his ankle lest he perish from the presence of God and need to be pulled out.

Could one overstate the significance of the ark? Hardly. How precious to us would be the manger in which Jesus was born? And the cross? If we had the very cross on which he was crucified, would we cherish it? You'd think so.

So we wonder why the Israelites didn't cherish the ark of the covenant. Stunningly, they let it gather dust for thirty years in the house of a priest who lived seven miles west of Jerusalem. Neglected. Ignored. But just-crowned David determines to change that. After he settles the city of Jerusalem, he makes the return of the chest his top priority. He plans a Macy's-caliber parade and invites thirty thousand Hebrews to attend.

They gather near the home of Abinadab, the priest. His two sons,[1] Uzzah and Ahio, are put in charge of the transport. They load the ark on an ox-drawn wagon and begin the march. Trumpets blast, songs erupt, and all goes well for the first two miles, until they hit a patch of rough road. The oxen stumble, the wagon shakes, and the ark shifts. Uzzah, thinking the holy chest is about to fall off the wagon, extends his hand to steady it. And heaven Uzied Uzzah, and "and he died" (2 Sam. 6:7).

This will dampen a parade real quick. Everyone goes home. Deeply distressed, David returns to Jerusalem. The ark is kept at the home of Obed-Edom while David sorts things out. Apparently, he succeeds, because at the end of three months David returns, reclaims the ark, and resumes the parade. This time there is no death. There is dancing. David enters Jerusalem with rejoicing. And "David danced before the LORD with all his might" (6:14).

Two men. One dead. The other dancing. What do they teach us? Specifically, what do they teach us about invoking the presence of God? This is what David wants to know: "How can the ark of the Lord come to me?" (6:9).

Uzzah's tragedy teaches this: God comes on his own terms.

In the story of David and his giants, this is one giant-size issue. Is God a distant deity? Mothers ask, "How can the presence of God come over my children?" Fathers ponder, "How can God's presence fill my house?" Churches desire the touching, helping, healing presence of God in their midst.

How can the presence of God come to us?

Should we light a candle, sing chants, build an altar, head up a committee, give a barrelful of money? What invokes the presence of God? Uzzah and David blend death and dancing to reveal an answer.

Uzzah's tragedy teaches this: *God comes on his own terms.* He gave specific instructions as to the care and transport of the ark. Only the priests could draw near it. And then only after they had offered sacrifices for themselves and their families (see Lev. 16). The ark would be lifted, not with hands, but with acacia poles. Priests ran long rods through the rings on the corners to carry the ark. "The Kohathites will come and carry these things to the next destination. But they must not touch the sacred objects, or they will die. . . . they were required to carry the sacred objects of the Tabernacle on their shoulders" (Num. 4:15; 7:9 NLT).

Uzzah should have known this. He was a priest, a Koathite priest, a descendant of Aaron himself. The ark had been kept in the house of his father, Abinadab. He had grown up with it. Which may be the best explanation for his actions.

He gets word that the king wants the chest and says, "Sure, I can get it. We keep it out back in the barn. Let's load it up." The holy has become humdrum. The sacred, second-rate. So he exchanges commands for convenience, using a wagon instead of poles and bulls instead of priests. We see no obedience or sacrifice; we see expediency.

God is angered.

But did he have to kill Uzzah? Did he have to take his life?

We posed the question to Joe Shulam. Joe grew up Jerusalem, studied at the Orthodox Jewish Rabbinical Seminary, and still lives in Israel. He deeply understands the Old Testament. He met a group of us at the airport and drove us to Jerusalem, passing near the place where Uzzah was slain. "The question," Joe opined in response, "is not why did God kill Uzzah but rather why does he let us live?"

Judging from the number of dead churches and cold hearts, I'm not so sure he does.

Distant Deity

The image of a dead Uzzah sends a sobering and shuddering reminder to those of us who can attend church as often as we wish, take communion anytime we desire. The message: don't grow lax before the holy. God won't be loaded on convenient wagons or toted about by dumb animals. Don't confuse him with a genie who pops out at the rub of a lamp or a butler who appears at the ring of a bell.

Don't grow lax before the holy.

God comes, mind you. But he comes on his own terms. He comes when commands are revered, hearts are clean, and confession is made.

But what of the second figure? What is the message of one man dancing?

David's initial response to the slaying of Uzzah is anything but joyful. He retreats to Jerusalem, confused and hurt, "angry because the Lord had punished Uzzah in his anger" (1 Chron. 13:11 NCV). Three months pass before David returns for the ark. He does so with a different protocol. Priests replace bulls. Sacrifice replaces convenience. Levites prepare "themselves for service to the Lord." They use "special poles to carry the Ark of God on their shoulders, as Moses had commanded, just as the Lord had said they should" (1 Chron. 15:14–15 NCV).

No one hurries. "And so it was, when those bearing the ark of the Lord had gone six paces, that he [David] sacrificed oxen and fatted sheep" (2 Sam. 6:13). When David realizes that God is not angry, he offers a sacrifice and _____. Select the correct answer from the following:

a. kneels before the Lord
b. falls prostrate before the Lord
c. bows his head before the Lord
d. dances with all his might before the Lord

If you answered *d*, you win a pass to the church square dance. David dances mightily before the Lord (6:14). Somersaults, high kicks. Spinning, jumping. This is no tapping of the feet or swaying of the head. The Hebrew term portrays David rotating in circles, hopping and springing. Forget token shuffle or obligatory waltz. David-the-giant-killer becomes David-the-two-stepper. He's the mayor of Dublin on Saint Patrick's Day, hopping and bopping at the head of the parade.

God comes when commands are revered,
hearts are clean, and confession is made.

And, if that's not enough, he strips down to the ephod, the linen prayer vest. It covers the same amount of territory as a long T-shirt. Right there in front of God and the altar and everyone else, David removes all but his holy skivvies. (Envision the president escaping the Oval Office and cartwheeling down Pennsylvania Avenue in his Fruit of the Looms.)

David dances and we duck. We hold our breath. We know what's coming. We read about Uzzah. We know what God does to the irreverent and cocky. Apparently, David wasn't paying attention. For here he is, in the full presence of God and God's children, doing a jig in his undergarment. Hold your breath and call the undertaker. So long, King David. Prepare to be fried, flambéed, and fricasseed.

But nothing happens. The sky is silent, and David keeps twirling, and we are left wondering. Doesn't the dance bother God? What does David have that Uzzah didn't? Why isn't the heavenly Father angered?

For the same reason I wasn't. They don't do it now, but when my daughters were toddlers, they would dance when I came home. My car in the driveway was their signal to strike up the band. "Daddy's here!" they'd declare, bursting through the door. Right there in the front lawn they would dance. Flamboyantly. With chocolate on their faces and diapers on their bottoms, they would promenade about for all the neighbors to see.

Did it bother me? Was I angered? Was I concerned what people would think? Did I tell them to straighten up and act mature? Absolutely not.

Did God tell David to behave? No. He let him dance.

Scripture doesn't portray David dancing at any other time. He did no death dance over Goliath. He never scooted the boot among the Philistines. He didn't inaugurate his term as king with a waltz or dedicate Jerusalem with a ballroom swirl. But when God came to town, he couldn't sit still.

Maybe God wonders how we do. Do we not enjoy what David wanted? The presence of God. Jesus promised, "I am with you always, even to the end of the age" (Matt. 28:20). Yet, how long since we rolled back the rug and celebrated the night away because of it?

What did David know that we don't? What did he remember that we forget? In a sentence, it might be this:

God's present is his presence.

His greatest gift is himself. Sunsets steal our breath. Caribbean blue stills our hearts. Newborn babies stir our tears. Lifelong love bejewels our lives. But take all these away—strip away the sunsets, oceans, cooing babies, and tender hearts—and leave us in the Sahara, and we still have reason to dance in the sand. Why? Because God is with us.

God's present is his presence. His greatest gift is himself.

This must be what David knew. And this must be what God wants us to know. We are never alone. Ever.

God loves you too much to leave you alone, so he hasn't. He hasn't left you alone with your fears, your worries, your disease, or your death. So kick up your heels for joy.

And party! David "blessed the people in the name of the LORD Almighty. Then he gave a gift of food to every man and woman in Israel: a loaf of bread, a cake of dates, and a cake of raisins" (2 Sam. 6:18–19 NLT). God is with us. That's reason to celebrate.

Uzzah, it seems, missed this. Uzzah had a view of a small god, a god who fit in a box and needed help with his balance. So Uzzah didn't prepare for him. He didn't purify himself to encounter the holy: no sacrifice offered, no commandments observed. Forget the repentance and obedience; load God in the back of the wagon, and let's get going.

Or, in our case, live like hell for six days and cash in on Sunday grace. Or who cares what you believe; just wear a cross around your neck for good luck. Or light a few candles and say a few prayers and get God on your side.

Uzzah's lifeless body cautions against such irreverence. No awe of God leads to the death of man. God won't be cajoled, commanded, conjured up, or called down. He is a personal God who loves and heals and helps and intervenes. He doesn't respond to magic potions or clever slogans. He looks for more. He looks for reverence, obedience, and God-hungry hearts.

And when he sees them, he comes! And when he comes, let the band begin. And, yes, a reverent heart and a dancing foot can belong to the same person.

David had both.

May we have the same.

A reverent heart and a dancing foot can belong to the same person.

By the way, remember what I said about my daughters dancing with diapers and big smiles? I used to dance with them. You think I'd sit on the side and miss the fun? No sirree, Bob. I'd sweep them up—two, even three at a time—and around we'd twirl. No father misses the chance to dance with his child.

(Which makes me wonder if David might have had a dancing partner.)

14

TOUGH PROMISES

K ING DAVID'S life couldn't be better. Just crowned. His throne room smells like fresh paint, and his city architect is laying out new neighborhoods. God's ark indwells the tabernacle; gold and silver overflow the king's coffers; Israel's enemies maintain their distance. The days of ducking Saul are a distant memory.

But something stirs one of them. A comment, perhaps, resurrects an old conversation. Maybe a familiar face jars a dated decision. In the midst of his new life, David remembers a promise from his old one: "Is there still anyone who is left of the house of Saul, that I may show him kindness for Jonathan's sake?" (2 Sam. 9:1).

Confusion furrows the faces of David's court. Why bother with the children of Saul? This is a new era, a new administration. Who cares about the old guard? David does. He does because he remembers the covenant he made with Jonathan. When Saul threatened to kill David, Jonathan sought to save him. Jonathan succeeded and then made this request: "If I make it through this alive, continue to be my covenant friend. And if I die, keep the covenant friendship with my family—forever" (1 Sam. 20:14–15 MSG).

Jonathan does die. But David's covenant does not. No one would have thought twice had he let it. David has many reasons to forget the vow he made with Jonathan.

The two were young and idealistic. Who keeps the promises of youth?

Saul was cruel and relentless. Who honors the children of a nemesis?

David has a nation to rule and an army to lead. What king has time for small matters?

But, to David, a covenant is no small matter. When you catalog the giants David faced, be sure the word *promise* survives the cut and makes the short list. It certainly appears on most lists of Everestish challenges.

The husband of a depressed wife knows the challenge of a promise. As she daily stumbles through a gloomy fog, he wonders what happened to the girl he married. Can you keep a promise in a time like this?

The wife of a cheating husband asks the same. He's back. He's sorry. She's hurt. She wonders, *He broke his promise. . . . Do I keep mine?*

Parents have asked such a question. Parents of prodigals. Parents of runaways. Parents of the handicapped and disabled.

Even parents of healthy toddlers have wondered how to keep a promise. Honeymoon moments and quiet evenings are buried beneath the mountain of dirty diapers and short nights.

Promises. Pledged amidst spring flowers. Cashed in February grayness. They loom Gulliver-size over our Lilliputian lives. We never escape their shadow. David, it seems, didn't attempt to.

Promises. Pledged amidst spring flowers.
Cashed in February grayness.

Finding a descendant of Jonathan wasn't easy. No one in David's circle knew one. Advisers summoned Ziba, a former servant of Saul. Did he know of a surviving member of Saul's household? Take a good look at Ziba's answer: "Yes, one of Jonathan's sons is still alive, but he is crippled" (2 Sam. 9:3 NLT).

Ziba mentions no name, just points out that the boy is lame. We sense a thinly veiled disclaimer in his words. "Be careful, David. He isn't—how would you say it?—suited for the palace. You might think twice about keeping this promise."

Ziba gives no details about the boy, but the fourth chapter of 2 Samuel does. The person in question is the son of Jonathan, Mephibosheth. (What great names! Needing ideas on what to name your newborns? Try Ziba and Mephibosheth. They'll stand out in their class.)

When Mephibosheth was five years old, his father and grandfather died at the hands of the Philistines. Knowing their brutality, the family of Saul headed for the hills. Mephibosheth's nurse snatched him up and ran, then tripped and dropped the boy, breaking both his ankles, leaving him incurably lame. Escaping servants carried him across the Jordan River to an inhospitable village called Lo Debar. The name means "without pasture." Picture a tumbleweed-tossed, low-rent trailer town in an Arizona desert. Mephibosheth hid there, first for fear of the Philistines, then for fear of David.

Collect the sad details of Mephibosheth's life:

- born rightful heir to the throne
- victimized by a fall
- left with halting feet in a foreign land
- where he lived under the threat of death.

Victimized. Ostracized. Disabled. Uncultured.

"Are you sure?" Ziba's reply insinuates, "Are you sure you want the likes of this boy in your palace?"

David is sure.

Servants drive a stretch limousine across the Jordan River and knock on the door of the shack. They explain their business, load Mephibosheth into the car, and carry him into the palace. The boy assumes the worst. He enters the presence of David with the enthusiasm of a death-row inmate entering the lethal injection room.

The boy bows low and asks,

"Who am I that you pay attention to a stray dog like me?"

David then called in Ziba, Saul's right-hand man, and told him, "Everything that belonged to Saul and his family, I've handed over to your master's grandson. . . . from now on [he] will take all his meals at my table." (9:8–10 MSG)

Faster than you can say Mephibosheth twice, he gets promoted from Lo Debar to the king's table. Good-bye, obscurity. Hello, royalty and realty. Note: David could have sent money to Lo Debar. A lifelong annuity would have generously fulfilled his promise. But David gave Mephibosheth more than a pension; he gave him a place—a place at the royal table.

Look closely at the family portrait hanging over David's fireplace; you'll see the grinning graduate of Lo Debar High School. David sits enthroned in the center, flanked by far too many wives. Just in front of tanned and handsome Absalom, right next to the drop-dead beauty of Tamar, down the row from bookish Solomon, you'll see Mephibosheth, the grandson of Saul, the son of Jonathan, leaning on his crutches and smiling as if he's just won the Jerusalem lottery.

Which indeed he had. The kid who had no legs to stand on has everything to live for. Why? Because he impressed David? Convinced David? Coerced David? No, Mephibosheth did nothing. A promise prompted David. The king is kind, not because the boy is deserving, but because the promise is enduring.

For further proof, follow the life of Mephibosheth. He beds down in the bastion and disappears from Scripture for fifteen years or so. He resurfaces amidst the drama of Absalom's rebellion.

Absalom, a rebellious curse of a kid, forces David to flee Jerusalem. The king escapes in disgrace with only a few faithful friends. Guess who is numbered among them. Mephibosheth? I thought you'd think so. But he isn't. Ziba is. Ziba tells David that Mephibosheth has sided with the enemy. The story progresses, and Absalom perishes, and David returns to Jerusalem, where Mephibosheth gives the king another version of the story. He meets David wearing a ragged beard and dirty clothing. Ziba, he claims, abandoned him in Jerusalem and would not place him on a horse so he could travel.

Who's telling the truth? Ziba or Mephibosheth? One is lying. Which one? We don't know. We don't know because David never asks. He never asks, because it doesn't matter. If Mephibosheth tells the truth, he stays. If he lies, he stays. His place in the palace depends, not on his behavior, but on David's promise.

God sets the standard for covenant keeping.

Why? Why is David so loyal? And how? How is David so loyal? Mephibosheth brings nothing and takes much. From whence does David quarry such resolve? Were we able to ask David how he fulfilled his giant-of-a-promise, he would take us from his story to God's story. God sets the standard for covenant keeping.

As Moses told the Israelites:

Know this: God, your God, is God indeed, a God you can depend upon. He keeps his covenant of loyal love with those who love him and observe his commandments for a thousand generations. (Deut. 7:9 MSG)

God makes and never breaks his promises. The Hebrew word for covenant, *beriyth*, means "a solemn agreement with binding force."[1] His irrevocable covenant runs like a scarlet thread through the tapestry of Scripture. Remember his promise to Noah?

"I establish my covenant with you: Never again will all life be cut off by the waters of a flood; never again will there be a flood to destroy the earth."

And God said, "This is the sign of the covenant I am making between me and you and every living creature with you, a covenant for all generations to come: I have set my rainbow in the clouds, and it will be the sign of the covenant between me and the earth." (Gen. 9:11–13 NIV)

Every rainbow reminds us of God's covenant. Curiously, astronauts who've seen rainbows from outer space tell us they form a complete circle.[2] God's promises are equally unbroken and unending.

---

*God's irrevocable covenant runs like
a scarlet thread through the tapestry of Scripture.*

Abraham can tell you about promises. God told this patriarch that counting the stars and counting his descendants would be equal challenges. To secure the oath, God had Abraham cut several animals in half. To seal a covenant in the Ancient East, the promise-maker passed between a divided animal carcass, volunteering to meet the same fate if he broke his word.

As the sun went down and it became dark, Abram saw a smoking firepot and a flaming torch pass between the halves of the carcasses. So the LORD made a covenant with Abram that day and said, "I have given this land to your descendants, all the way from the border of Egypt to the great Euphrates River." (Gen. 15:17–18 NLT)

God takes promises seriously and seals them dramatically. Consider the case of Hosea. Seven hundred years before the birth of Jesus, God commanded Hosea to marry a prostitute named Gomer. (If her profession didn't get you, her name would.) Still, Hosea obeyed. Gomer gave birth to three children, none of whom were Hosea's. Gomer abandoned Hosea for a life equivalent to a call girl at a strip club. Rock bottom came in the form of an auction pit, where men bid on her as a slave. Lesser men would have waved her off. Not Hosea. He jumped into the bidding and bought his wife and took her home again. Why? Here's Hosea's explanation.

> Then GOD ordered me, "Start all over: Love your wife again,
>> your wife who's in bed with her latest boyfriend, your cheating wife.
>> Love her the way I, God, love the Israelite people,
>> even as they flirt and party with every god that takes their fancy."
>> I did it. I paid good money to get her back.
>> It cost me the price of a slave. (Hos. 3:1–2 MSG)

Need a picture of our promise-keeping God? Look at Hosea buying back his wife. Look at the smoldering pot passing between the animals. Look at the rainbow. Or look at Mephibosheth. You've never introduced yourself as Mephibosheth from Lo Debar, but you could. Remember the details of his disaster? He was

- born rightful heir to the throne,
- victimized by a fall, and
- left with halting feet in a foreign land,
- where he lived under the threat of death.

That's your story! Were you not born as a child of the King? Have you not been left hobbling because of the stumble of Adam and Eve? Who among us hasn't meandered along the dry sand of Lo Debar?

But then came the palace messenger. A fourth-grade teacher, a high school buddy, an aunt, a television preacher. They came with big news and an awaiting limo. "You are not going to believe this," they announced, "but the King of Israel has a place for you at the table. The place card is printed, and the chair is empty. He wants you in his family."

Your eternal life is covenant caused, covenant secured, and covenant based.

Why? Because of your IQ? God needs no counsel.

Your retirement account? Not worth a dime to God.

Your organizational skills? Sure. The architect of orbits needs your advice.

Sorry, Mephibosheth. Your invitation has nothing to do with you and everything to do with God. He made a promise to give you eternal life: "God, who never lies, promised this eternal life before the world began" (Titus 1:2 GOD's WORD).

Your eternal life is covenant caused, covenant secured, and

covenant based. You can put Lo Debar in the rearview mirror for one reason—God keeps his promises. Shouldn't God's promise-keeping inspire yours?

Heaven knows you could use some inspiration. People can exhaust you. And there are times when all we can do is not enough. When a spouse chooses to leave, we cannot force him or her to stay. When a spouse abuses, we shouldn't stay. The best of love can go unrequited. I don't for a moment intend to minimize the challenges some of you face. You're tired. You're angry. You're disappointed. This isn't the marriage you expected or the life you wanted. But looming in your past is a promise you made. May I urge you to do all you can to keep it? To give it one more try?

Why should you? So you can understand the depth of God's love.

---

*When you love the unloving,
you get a glimpse of what God does for you.*

When you love the unloving, you get a glimpse of what God does for you. When you keep the porch light on for the prodigal child, when you do what is right even though you have been done wrong, when you love the weak and the sick, you do what God does every single moment. Covenant-keeping enrolls you in the post-graduate school of God's love.

Is this why God has given you this challenge? When you love liars, cheaters, and heartbreakers, are you not doing what God has done for us? Pay attention to and take notes on your struggles. God invites you to understand his love.

He also wants you to illustrate it.

David did with Mephibosheth. David was a walking parable of God's loyalty. Hosea did the same with Gomer. He wardrobed divine devotion. My mother did with my father. I remember watching her care for him in his final months. ALS had sucked life from every muscle in his body. She did for him what mothers do for infants. She bathed, fed, and dressed him. She placed a hospital bed in the den of our house and made him her mission. If she complained, I never heard it. If she frowned, I never saw it. What I heard and saw was a covenant keeper. "This is what love does," her actions announced as she powdered his body, shaved his face, and washed his sheets. She modeled the power of a promise kept.

God calls on you to do the same. Illustrate stubborn love. Incarnate fidelity. God is giving you a Mephibosheth-size chance to show your children and your neighbors what real love does.

Embrace it. Who knows? Someone may tell your story of loyalty to illustrate the loyalty of God.

One final thought. Remember the family portrait in David's palace? I doubt if David had one. But I think heaven might. Won't it be great to see your face in the picture? Sharing the frame with folks like Moses and Martha, Peter and Paul . . . there will be you and Mephibosheth.

He won't be the only one grinning.

15

THIN AIR-OGANCE

YOU CAN CLIMB too high for your own good. It's possible to ascend too far, stand too tall, and elevate too much.

Linger too long at high altitudes, and two of your senses suffer. Your hearing dulls. It's hard to hear people when you are higher than they. Voices grow distant. Sentences seem muffled. And when you are up there, your eyesight dims. It's hard to focus on people when you are so far above them. They appear so small. Little figures with no faces. You can hardly distinguish one from the other. They all look alike.

You don't hear them. You don't see them. You are above them.

Which is exactly where David is. He has never been higher. The wave of his success crests at age fifty. Israel is expanding. The country is prospering. In two decades on the throne, he has distinguished himself as a warrior, musician, statesman, and king. His cabinet is strong, and his boundaries stretch for sixty thousand square miles. No defeats on the battlefield. No blemishes on his administration. Loved by the people. Served by the soldiers. Followed by the crowds. David is at an all-time high.

You can climb too high for your own good.

Quite a contrast to how we first found him in the Valley of Elah: kneeling at the brook, searching for five smooth stones. All others stood. The soldiers stood. Goliath stood. His brothers stood. The others were high; David was low, belly down in the lowest part of the valley. Never lower, yet never stronger.

Three decades later his situation is reversed. Never higher, yet never weaker. David stands at the highest point of his life, in the highest position in the kingdom, at the highest place in the city—on the balcony overlooking Jerusalem.

He should be with his men, at battle, astride his steed and against his foe. But he isn't. He is at home.

> In the spring, when the kings normally went out to war, David sent out Joab, his servants, and all the Israelites. They destroyed the Ammonites and attacked the city of Rabbah. But David stayed in Jerusalem. (2 Sam. 11:1 NCV)

It's springtime in Israel. The nights are warm, and the air is sweet. David has time on his hands, love on his mind, and people at his disposal.

His eyes fall upon a woman as she bathes. We'll always wonder if Bathsheba was bathing in a place where she shouldn't bathe, hoping David would look where he shouldn't look. We'll never know. But we know that he looks and likes what he sees. So he inquires about her. A servant returns with this information: "That woman is Bathsheba daughter of Eliam. She is the wife of Uriah the Hittite" (11:3 NCV).

The servant laces his information with a warning. He gives not only the woman's name but her marital status and the name of her husband. Why tell David she is married if not to caution him? And why give the husband's name unless David is familiar with it?

Odds are, David knew Uriah. The servant hopes to deftly dissuade the king. But David misses the hint. The next verse describes his first step down a greasy slope. "So David sent messengers to bring Bathsheba to him. When she came to him, he had sexual relations with her" (11:4 NCV).

David "sends" many times in this story. He *sends* Joab to battle (v. 1). He *sends* the servant to inquire about Bathsheba (v. 3). He *sends* for Bathsheba to have her come to him (v. 4). When David learns of her pregnancy, he *sends* word to Joab (v. 6) to *send* Uriah back to Jerusalem. David *sends* him to Bathsheba to rest, but Uriah is too noble. David opts to *send* Uriah back to a place in the battle where he is sure to be killed. Thinking his cover-up is complete, David *sends* for Bathsheba and marries her (v. 27).

We don't like this sending, demanding David. We prefer the pastoring David, caring for the flock; the dashing David, hiding from Saul; the worshiping David, penning psalms. We aren't prepared for the David who has lost control of his self-control, who sins as he sends.

What has happened to him? Simple. Altitude sickness. He's been too high too long. The thin air has messed with his senses. He can't hear as he used to. He can't hear the warnings of the servant or the voice of his conscience. Nor can he hear his Lord. The pinnacle has dulled his ears and blinded his eyes. Did David see Bathsheba? No. He saw Bathsheba bathing. He saw Bathsheba's body and Bathsheba's curves. He saw Bathsheba, the conquest. But did he see Bathsheba, the human being? The wife of Uriah? The daughter of Israel? The creation of God? No. David had lost his vision. Too long at the top will do that to you. Too many hours in the bright sun and thin air leaves you breathless and dizzy.

Linger too long at high altitudes, and . . .
your hearing dulls. . . . [and] your eyesight dims.

Of course, who among us could ever ascend as high as David? Who among us is a finger snap away from a rendezvous with anyone we choose? Presidents and kings might send people to do their bidding; we're lucky to send out for Chinese food. We don't have that kind of clout.

We can understand David's other struggles. His fear of Saul. Long stretches hiding in the wilderness. We've been there. But David high and mighty? David's balcony is one place we've never been.

Or have we?

I wasn't on a balcony, but I was on a flight. And I didn't watch a woman bathe, but I did watch an airline attendant fumble. She couldn't do anything right. Order soda, and she'd bring juice. Ask for a pillow, and she'd bring a blanket, if she brought anything at all.

And I started to grumble. Not out loud, but in my thoughts. *What's the matter with service these days?* I suppose I was feeling a bit smug. I'd just been a guest speaker at an event. People had told me how lucky they were that I had come. I don't know what was loonier: the fact that they said it or that I believed it. So I boarded the plane feeling cocky. I had to tilt my head to enter the doorway. I took my seat knowing the flight was safe, since heaven knows, I'm essential to the work of God.

Then I asked for the soda, the pillow. . . . She blew the assignments, and I growled. Do you see what I was doing? Placing myself higher than the airline attendant. In the pecking order of the plane, she was below me. Her job was to serve, and my job was to be served.

Don't look at me like that. Haven't you felt a bit superior to someone? A parking lot attendant. The clerk at the grocery store. The peanut-seller at the game. The employee at the coat check. You've done what I did. And we've done what David did. We've lost our sight and hearing.

When I looked at the airline attendant, I didn't see a human being; I saw a necessary commodity. But her question changed all that.

"Mr. Lucado?" Imagine my surprise when the airline attendant knelt beside my seat. "Are you the one who writes the Christian books?"

Christian books, yes. Christian thoughts—that's another matter, I said to myself, descending the balcony stairs.

"May I talk to you?" she asked. Her eyes misted, and her heart opened, and she filled the next three or four minutes with her pain. Divorce papers had arrived that morning. Her husband wouldn't return her calls. She didn't know where she was going to live. She could hardly focus on work. Would I pray for her?

I did. But both God and I knew she was not the only one needing prayer.

Perhaps you could use a prayer too? How is your hearing? Do you hear the servants whom God sends? Do you hear the conscience that God stirs?

And your vision? Do you still see people? Or do you see only their functions? Do you see people who need you, or do you see people beneath you?

The story of David and Bathsheba is less a story of lust and more a story of power. A story of a man who rose too high for his own good. A man who needed to hear these words: "Come down before you fall."

---

*David and Bathsheba: less a story of lust
and more a story of power.*

"First pride, then the crash—the bigger the ego, the harder the fall" (Prov. 16:18 MSG).

This must be why God hates arrogance. He hates to see his children fall. He hates to see his Davids seduce and his Bathshebas be victimized. God hates what pride does to his children. He doesn't dislike arrogance. He hates it. Could he state it any clearer than Proverbs 8:13: "I hate pride and arrogance" (NIV)? And then a few chapters later: "God can't stomach arrogance or pretense; believe me, he'll put those upstarts in their place" (16:5 MSG).

You don't want God to do that. Just ask David. He never quite recovered from his bout with this giant. Don't make his mistake. 'Tis far wiser to descend the mountain than fall from it.

Pursue humility. Humility doesn't mean you think less of yourself but that you think of yourself less. "Don't cherish exaggerated ideas of yourself or your importance, but try to have a sane estimate of your capabilities by the light of the faith that God has given to you" (Rom. 12:3 PHILLIPS).

> *Humility doesn't mean you think less of yourself but that you think of yourself less.*

Embrace your poverty. We're all equally broke and blessed. "People come into this world with nothing, and when they die they leave with nothing" (Eccles. 5:15 NCV).

Resist the place of celebrity. "Go sit in a seat that is not important. When the host comes to you, he may say, 'Friend, move up here to a more important place.' Then all the other guests will respect you" (Luke 14:10 NCV).

Wouldn't you rather be invited up than put down?

God has a cure for the high and mighty: come down from the mountain. You'll be amazed what you hear and who you see. And you'll breathe a whole lot easier.

16

COLOSSAL COLLAPSES

WHAT WILL THE Vatican give for the pope's name? Rogers Cadenhead sought an answer. Upon the death of Pope John Paul, this self-described "domain hoarder" registered www.Benedict XVI.com before the new pope's name was announced. Cadenhead secured it before Rome knew they needed it.

The right domain name can prove lucrative. Another name, www.PopeBenedictXVI.com, surpassed sixteen thousand dollars on E-bay. Cadenhead, however, didn't want money. A Catholic himself, he's happy for the church to own the name. "I'm going to try and avoid angering 1.1 billion Catholics and my grandmother," he quipped.

He would like something in return though. In exchange, Cadenhead sought

1. "one of those hats";
2. "a free stay at the Vatican hotel"; and
3. "complete absolution, no questions asked, for the third week of March 1987."[1]

Makes you wonder what happened that week, doesn't it? It may remind you of a week of your own. Most of us have one or more.

A folly-filled summer, a month off track, days gone wild. If a box of tapes existed documenting every second of your life, which tapes would you burn? Do you have a season in which you indulged, imbibed, or inhaled?

King David did. Could a collapse be more colossal than his? He seduces and impregnates Bathsheba, murders her husband, and deceives his general and soldiers. Then he marries her. She bears the child.

The cover-up appears complete. The casual observer detects no cause for concern. David has a new wife and a happy life. All seems well on the throne. But all is not well in David's heart. Guilt simmers. He will later describe this season of secret sin in graphic terms:

> When I kept it all inside,
>> my bones turned to powder,
>> my words became daylong groans.
>
> The pressure never let up;
>> all the juices of my life dried up. (Ps. 32:3–4 MSG)

David's soul resembles a Canadian elm in winter. Barren. Fruit-less. Gray-shrouded. His harp hangs unstrung. His hope hibernates. The guy is a walking wreck. His "third week of March" stalks him like a pack of wolves. He can't escape it. Why? Because God keeps bringing it up.

Underline the last verse of 2 Samuel chapter 11: "The thing that David had done displeased the Lord" (v. 27). With these words the narrator introduces a new character into the David and Bathsheba drama: God. Thus far, he's been absent from the text, unmentioned in the story.

David seduces—no mention of God. David plots—no mention of God. Uriah buried, Bathsheba married—no mention of God. God is not spoken to and does not speak. The first half of verse 27 lures the reader into a faux happy ending: Bathsheba "became David's wife and gave birth to his son" (NCV). They decorate the nursery and pick names out of a magazine. Nine months pass. A son is born. And we conclude: David dodged a bullet. Angels dropped this story into the file marked "Boys will be boys." God turned a blind eye. Yet, just when we think so and David hopes so . . . Some-one steps from behind the curtain and takes center stage. "The thing that David had done displeased the LORD."

God will be silent no more. The name not mentioned until the final verse of chapter 11 dominates chapter 12. David, the "sender," sits while God takes control.

God sends Nathan to David. Nathan is a prophet, a preacher, a White House chaplain of sorts. The man deserves a medal for going to the king. He knows what happened to Uriah. David had killed an innocent soldier . . . What will he do with a confronting preacher?

Still, Nathan goes. Rather than declare the deed, he relates a story about a poor man with one sheep. David instantly connects. He shepherded flocks before he led people. He knows poverty. He's the youngest son of a family too poor to hire a shepherd. Nathan tells David how the poor shepherd loved this sheep—holding her in his own lap, feeding her from his own plate. She was all he had.

Enter, as the story goes, the rich jerk. A traveler stops by his mansion, so a feast is in order. Rather than slaughter a sheep from his own flock, the rich man sends his bodyguards to steal the poor man's animal. They Hummer onto his property, snatch the lamb, and fire up the barbecue.

As David listens, hair rises on his neck. He grips the arms of the throne. He renders a verdict without a trial: fish bait by nightfall. "The man who has done this shall surely die! And he shall restore fourfold for the lamb, because he did this thing and because he had no pity" (12:5–6).

Oh, David. You never saw it coming, did you? You never saw Nathan erecting the gallows or throwing the rope over the beam. You never felt him tie your hands behind your back, lead you up the steps, and stand you squarely over the trap door. Only when he squeezed the noose around your neck, did you gulp. Only when Nathan tightened the rope with four three-letter words:

"You are the man!" (12:7).

David's face pales; his Adam's apple bounces. A bead of sweat forms on his forehead. He slinks back in his chair. He makes no defense. He utters no response. He has nothing to say. God, however, is just clearing his throat. Through Nathan he proclaims:

> I made you king over Israel. I freed you from the fist of Saul. I gave you your master's daughter and other wives to have and to hold. I gave you both Israel and Judah. And if that hadn't been enough, I'd have gladly thrown in much more. So why have you treated the word of God with brazen contempt, doing this great evil? You murdered Uriah the Hittite, then took his wife as your wife. Worse, you killed him with an Ammonite sword! (12:7–9 MSG)

God's words reflect hurt, not hate; bewilderment, not belittlement. Your flock fills the hills. Why rob? Beauty populates your palace. Why take from someone else? Why would the wealthy steal? David has no excuse.

So God levies a sentence.

> Now, therefore, the sword will never depart from your house, because you despised me and took the wife of Uriah the Hittite to be your own.
>
> This is what the Lord says: "Out of your own household I am going to bring calamity upon you. Before your very eyes I will take your wives and give them to one who is close to you, and he will lie with your wives in broad daylight. You did it in secret, but I will do this thing in broad daylight before all Israel." (12:10–12 NIV)

From this day forward, turmoil and tragedy mark David's family. Even the child of this adultery will die (12:18). He must. Surrounding nations now question the holiness of David's God. David had soiled God's reputation, blemished God's honor. And God, who jealously guards his glory, punishes David's public sin in a public fashion. The infant perishes. The king of Israel discovers the harsh truth of Numbers 32:23: ". . . you can be sure that your sin will track you down" (MSG).

Have you found this to be true? Does your stubborn week of March 1987 hound you? Infect you? Colossal collapses won't leave us alone. They surface like a boil on the skin.

Can God sit idly as sin poisons his [children]?

My brother had one once. In his middle school years he contracted a case of the boils. Poisonous pus rose on the back of his neck like a tiny Mount St. Helens. My mom, a nurse, knew what the boil needed—a good squeezing. Two thumbs every morning. The more she pressed, the more he screamed. But she wouldn't stop until the seed of the boil popped out.

Gee, Max, thanks for the beautiful image.

I'm sorry to be so graphic, but I need to press this point. You think my mom was tough . . . Try the hands of God. Unconfessed sins sit on our hearts like festering boils, poisoning, expanding. And God, with gracious thumbs, applies the pressure:

The way of the transgressor is hard. (Prov. 13:15 ASV)

Those who plow evil and sow trouble reap evil and trouble. (Job 4:8 MSG)

God takes your sleep, your peace. He takes your rest. Want to know why? Because he wants to take away your sin. Can a mom do nothing as toxins invade her child? Can God sit idly as sin poisons his? He will not rest until we do what David did: confess our fault. "Then David said to Nathan, 'I have sinned against the Lord.' Nathan replied, 'The Lord has taken away your sin. You are not going to die'" (2 Sam. 12:13 NIV).

He will not rest until we do what David did: confess our fault.

Interesting. David sentenced the imaginary sheep stealer to death. God is more merciful. He put away David's sin. Rather than cover it up, he lifted it up and put it away. "As far as the east is from the west, so far has he removed our transgressions from us. As a father has compassion on his children, so the Lord has compassion on those who fear him" (Ps. 103:12–13 NIV).

Place the mistake before the judgment seat of God.
Let him condemn it, let him pardon it, and put it away.

It took David a year. It took a surprise pregnancy, the death of a soldier, the persuasion of a preacher, the probing and pressing of God, but David's hard heart finally softened, and he confessed: "I have sinned against the Lord" (2 Sam. 12:13).

And God did with the sin what he does with yours and mine—he put it away.

It's time for you to put your "third week of March 1987" to rest. Assemble a meeting of three parties: you, God, and your memory. Place the mistake before the judgment seat of God. Let him condemn it, let him pardon it, and let him put it away.

He will. And you don't have to own the pope's name for him to do so.

17

FAMILY MATTERS

D AVID LOOKS OLDER than his sixty-plus years. His shoulders
slump; his head hangs. He shuffles like an old man. He struggles
to place one foot in front of the other. He pauses often. Partly because
the hill is steep. Partly because he needs to weep.

This is the longest path he's ever walked. Longer than the one
from creekside to Goliath. Longer than the winding road from fugitive to king or the guilty road from conviction to confession. Those
trails bore some steep turns. But none compare with the ascent up
the Mount of Olives.

So David went up by the ascent of the Mount of Olives, and wept
as he went up; and he had his head covered and went barefoot.

And all the people who were with him covered their heads and went up, weeping as they went up. (2 Sam. 15:30)

Look carefully and you'll find the cause of David's tears. He wears no crown. His son Absalom has taken it by force. David has no home. Those walls rising to his back belong to the city of Jerusalem. He flees the capital he founded.

Who wouldn't weep at a time like this? No throne. No home. Jerusalem behind him and the wilderness ahead of him. What has happened? Did he lose a war? Was Israel ravaged by disease? Did famine starve his loved ones and drain his strength? How does a king end up old and lonely on an uphill path? Let's see if David will tell us. See how he responds to two simple questions.

David, how are things with your children?

He winces at the subject. Fourteen years have passed since David seduced Bathsheba, thirteen years since Nathan told David, "The sword shall never depart from your house" (2 Sam. 12:10).

Nathan's prophecy has proved painfully true. One of David's sons, Amnon, fell in lust with his half-sister Tamar, one of David's daughters by another marriage. Amnon pined, plotted, and raped her. After the rape, he discarded Tamar like a worn doll.

Tamar, understandably, came undone. She threw ashes on her head and tore the robe of many colors worn by virgin daughters of the king. She "remained desolate in her brother Absalom's house" (13:20). The next verse tells us David's response: "When King David heard of all these things, he was very angry."

That's it? That's all? We want a longer verse. We want a few verbs. *Confront* will do. *Punish* would be nice. *Banish* even better. We expect to read, "David was very angry and . . . *confronted* Amnon or *punished* Amnon or *banished* Amnon." But what did David do to Amnon?

Nothing. No lecture. No penalty. No imprisonment. No dressing down. No chewing out. David did nothing to Amnon.

And, even worse, he did nothing for Tamar. She needed his protection, his affirmation and validation. She needed a dad. What she got was silence. So Absalom, her brother, filled the void. He sheltered his sister and plotted against Amnon: got him drunk and had him killed.

Incest. Deceit. One daughter raped. One son dead. Another with blood on his hands. A palace in turmoil.

Again it was time for David to step up. Display his Goliath-killing courage, Saul-pardoning mercy, Brook-Besor leadership. David's family needed to see the best of David. But they saw none of David. He didn't intervene or respond. He wept. But wept in solitude.

Absalom interpreted the silence as anger and fled Jerusalem to hide in his grandfather's house. David made no attempt to see his son. For three years they lived in two separate cities. Absalom returned to Jerusalem, but David still refused to see him. Absalom married and had four children. "Absalom dwelt two full years in Jerusalem, but did not see the king's face" (14:28).

Such shunning could not have been easy. Jerusalem was a small town. Avoiding Absalom demanded daily plotting and spying. But David succeeded in neglecting his son.

More accurately, he neglected all his children. A passage from later in his life exposes his parenting philosophy. One of his sons, Adonijah, staged a coup. He assembled chariots and horsemen and personal bodyguards to take the throne. Did David object? Are you kidding? David "never crossed him at any time by asking, 'Why have you done so?'" (1 Kings 1:6 NASB).

David, the Homer Simpson of biblical dads. The picture of passivity. When we ask him about his kids, he just groans. When we ask him the second question, his face goes chalky.

David, how's your marriage?

We began to suspect trouble back in 2 Samuel chapter 3. What appears as dull genealogy is actually a parade of red flags.

> Sons were born to David at Hebron. The first was Amnon, whose mother was Ahinoam from Jezreel. The second son was Kileab, whose mother was Abigail, the widow of Nabal from Carmel. The third son was Absalom, whose mother was Maacah daughter of Talmai, the king of Geshur. The fourth son was Adonijah, whose mother was Haggith. The fifth son was Shephatiah, whose mother was Abital. The sixth son was Ithream, whose mother was Eglah, David's wife. These sons were born to David at Hebron. (vv. 2–5 NCV)

I count six wives. Add to this list Michal, his first wife, and Bathsheba, his most famous, and David had eight spouses—too many to give each one a day a week. The situation worsens as we uncover a passage buried in the family Bible of David. After listing the names of his sons, the genealogist adds, "These were all the sons of David, besides the sons of the concubines" (1 Chron. 3:9).

The concubines? David fathered other children through other mothers, and we don't even know how many. The cynical side of us wonders if David did. What was he thinking? Had he not read God's instruction: "A man shall leave his father and mother and be joined to his wife" (Gen. 2:24)? One man. One woman. One marriage. Simple addition. David opted for advanced trigonometry.

David did so much so well. He unified the twelve tribes into one nation. He masterminded military conquests. He founded the capital city and elevated God as the Lord of the people, bringing the ark to Jerusalem and paving the way for the temple. He wrote poetry we still read and psalms we still sing. But when it came to his family, David blew it.

Going AWOL on his family was David's greatest failure. Seducing Bathsheba was an inexcusable but explicable act of passion. Murdering Uriah was a ruthless yet predictable deed from a desperate heart. But passive parenting and widespread philandering? These were not sins of a slothful afternoon or the deranged reactions of self-defense. David's family foul-up was a lifelong stupor that cost him dearly.

Some years ago a young husband came to see me, proud that he had one wife at home and one lover in an apartment. He used David's infidelity to justify his own. He even said he was considering polygamy. After all, David was a polygamist.

The right response to such folly is, read the rest of the story.

Remember Absalom? David finally reunited with him, but it was too late. The seeds of bitterness had spread deep roots. Absalom resolved to overthrow his father. He recruited from David's army and staged a coup.

His takeover set the stage for the sad walk of David out of Jerusalem—up the Mount of Olives and into the wilderness. No crown. No city. Just a heavyhearted, lonely, old man. "So David went up by the ascent of the Mount of Olives, and wept as he went up; and he had his head covered and went barefoot" (2 Sam. 15:30).

Loyalists eventually chase Absalom down. When he tries to escape on horseback, his long hair tangles in a tree, and soldiers spear him. David hears the news and falls to pieces: "O my son Absalom—my son, my son Absalom—if only I had died in your place! O Absalom my son, my son!" (18:33).

Tardy tears. David succeeded everywhere except at home. And if you don't succeed at home, do you succeed at all? David would have benefited from the counsel of Paul the apostle: "And now a word to you fathers. Don't make your children angry by the way you treat them" (Eph. 6:4 NLT).

How do we explain David's disastrous home? How do we explain David's silence when it comes to his family? No psalms written about his children. Surely, out of all his wives, one was worthy of a sonnet or song. But he never talked about them.

Aside from the prayer he offered for Bathsheba's baby, Scripture gives no indication that he ever prayed for his family. He prayed about the Philistines, interceded for his warriors. He offered prayers for Jonathan, his friend, and for Saul, his archrival. But as far as his family is concerned, it's as if they never existed.

Was David too busy to notice them? Maybe. He had a city to settle and a kingdom to build.

Was he too important to care for them? "Let the wives raise the kids; I'll lead the nation."

Was he too guilty to shepherd them? After all, how could David, who had seduced Bathsheba and intoxicated and murdered Uriah, correct his sons when they raped and murdered?

Too busy. Too important. Too guilty. And now? Too late. A dozen exits too late. But it's not too late for you. Your home is your giant-size privilege, your towering priority. Do not make David's tragic mistake. How would you respond to the questions we asked him?

Your home is your giant-size privilege,
your towering priority.

How's your marriage?

Consider it your Testore cello. This finely constructed, seldom-seen instrument has reached the category of rare and is fast earning the status of priceless. Few musicians are privileged to play a Testore; even fewer are able to own one.

I happen to know a man who does. He, gulp, loaned it to me for a sermon. Wanting to illustrate the fragile sanctity of marriage, I asked him to place the nearly-three-centuries-old instrument on the stage, and I explained its worth to the church.

How do you think I treated the relic? Did I twirl it, flip it, and pluck the strings? No way. The cello is far too valuable for my clumsy fingers. Besides, its owner loaned it to me. I dared not dishonor his treasure.

On your wedding day, God loaned you his work of art: an intricately crafted, precisely formed masterpiece. He entrusted you with a one-of-a-kind creation. Value her. Honor him. Having been blessed with a Testore, why fiddle around with anyone else?

David missed this. He collected wives as trophies. He saw spouses as a means to his pleasure, not a part of God's plan. Don't make his mistake.

Be fiercely loyal to one spouse. *Fiercely* loyal. Don't even look twice at someone else. No flirting. No teasing. No loitering at her desk or lingering in his office. Who cares if you come across as rude or a prude? You've made a promise. Keep it.

---

*On your wedding day, God loaned you his work of art:
an intricately crafted, precisely formed masterpiece.*

And, as you do, nourish the children God gives.

How are things with your kids?

Quiet heroes dot the landscape of our society. They don't wear ribbons or kiss trophies; they wear spit-up and kiss boo-boos. They don't make the headlines, but they do sew the hemlines and check the outlines and stand on the sidelines. You won't find their names on the Nobel Prize short list, but you will find their names on the homeroom, carpool, and Bible teacher lists.

They are parents, both by blood and deed, name and calendar. Heroes. News programs don't call them. But that's okay. Because their kids do . . . They call them Mom. They call them Dad. And these moms and dads, more valuable than all the executives and lawmakers west of the Mississippi, quietly hold the world together.

Be numbered among them. Read books to your kids. Play ball while you can and they want you to. Make it your aim to watch every game they play, read every story they write, hear every recital in which they perform.

Children spell love with four letters: T-I-M-E. Not just quality time, but hang time, downtime, anytime, all the time. Your children are not your hobby; they are your calling.

Your spouse is not your trophy but your treasure.

Don't pay the price David paid. Can we flip ahead a few chapters to his final hours? To see the ultimate cost of a neglected family, look at the way our hero dies.

David is hours from the grave. A chill has set in that blankets can't remove. Servants decide he needs a person to warm him, someone to hold him tight as he takes his final breaths.

Children spell love with four letters: T-I-M-E.

Do they turn to one of his wives? No. Do they call on one of his children? No. They seek "for a lovely young woman throughout all the territory of Israel . . . and she cared for the king, and served him; but the king did not know her" (1 Kings 1:3–4).

I suspect that David would have traded all his conquered crowns for the tender arms of a wife. But it was too late. He died in the care of a stranger, because he made strangers out of his family.

But it's not too late for you.

Make your wife the object of your highest devotion. Make your husband the recipient of your deepest passion. Love the one who wears your ring.

And cherish the children who share your name.

Succeed at home first.

18

DASHED HOPES

"I HAD INTENDED . . .

The David who speaks the words is old. The hands that
swung the sling hang limp. The feet that danced before the ark now
shuffle. Though his eyes are still sharp, his hair is gray, and skin sags
beneath his beard.

"I had intended . . ."

A large throng listens. Courtiers, counselors, chamberlains, and
caretakers. They've assembled at David's command. The king is
tired. The time for his departure is near. They listen as he speaks.

"I had intended to build . . ."

Odd way to start a farewell speech. David mentions not what he
did but what he wanted to do, yet couldn't. "I had intended to build
a permanent home for the ark of the covenant of the LORD and for
the footstool of our God" (1 Chron. 28:2 NASB).

A temple. David had wanted to build a temple. What he had done for Israel, he wanted to do for the ark—protect it. What he had done with Jerusalem, he wanted to do with the temple—establish it. And who better than he to do so? Hadn't he, literally, written the book on worship? Didn't he rescue the ark of the covenant? The temple would have been his swan song, his signature deed. David had expected to dedicate his final years to building a shrine to God.

At least, that had been his intention. "I had intended to build a permanent home for the ark of the covenant of the LORD and for the footstool of our God. So I had made preparations to build it" (28:2 NASB).

Preparations. Architects chosen. Builders selected. Blueprints and plans, drawings and numbers. Temple columns sketched. Steps designed.

"I had intended . . . I had made preparations . . ."

Intentions. Preparations. But no temple. Why? Did David grow discouraged? No. He stood willing. Were the people resistant? Hardly. They gave generously. Were the resources scarce? Far from it. David "supplied more bronze than could be weighed, and . . . more cedar logs than could be counted" (1 Chron. 22:3–4 NCV). Then what happened?

A conjunction happened.

Conjunctions operate as the signal lights of sentences. Some, such as *and,* are green. Others, such as *however,* are yellow. A few are red. Sledgehammer red. They stop you. David got a red light.

I had made preparations to build it. *But* God said to me, "You shall not build a house for My name because you are a man of war and have shed blood. . . . Your son Solomon is the one who shall build My house and My courts." (1 Chron. 28:2–3, 6 NASB, emphasis mine)

David's bloodthirsty temperament cost him the temple privilege. All he could do was say:

I had intended . . .

    I had made preparations . . .

        But God . . .

I'm thinking of some people who have uttered similar words. God had different plans than they did.

One man waited until his midthirties to marry. Resolved to select the right spouse, he prayerfully took his time. When he found her, they moved westward, bought a ranch, and began their life together. After three short years, she was killed in an accident.

I had intended . . .

    I had made preparations . . .

        But God . . .

A young couple turned a room into a nursery. They papered walls, refinished a baby crib, but then the wife miscarried.

I had intended . . .

    I had made preparations . . .

        But God . . .

Willem wanted to preach. By the age of twenty-five, he'd experienced enough life to know he was made for the ministry. He sold art, taught language, traded in books; he could make a living, but it wasn't a life. His life was in the church. His passion was with the people.

So his passion took him to the coalfields of southern Belgium. There, in the spring of 1879, this Dutchman began to minister to the simple, hardworking miners of Borinage. Within weeks his passion was tested. A mining disaster injured scores of villagers. Willem nursed the wounded and fed the hungry; even scraping the slag heaps to give his people fuel.

After the rubble was cleared and the dead were buried, the young preacher had earned a place in their hearts. The tiny church overflowed with people hungry for his simple messages of love. Young Willem was doing what he'd always dreamed of doing.

But . . .

What do you do with the "but God" moments in life?

One day his superior came to visit. Willem's lifestyle shocked him. The young preacher wore an old soldier's coat. His trousers were cut from sacking, and he lived in a simple hut. Willem had given his salary to the people. The church official was unimpressed. "You look more pitiful than the people you came to teach," he said. Willem asked if Jesus wouldn't have done the same. The older man would have none of it. This was not the proper appearance for a minister. He dismissed Willem from the ministry.

The young man was devastated.

He only wanted to build a church. He only wanted to honor God. Why wouldn't God let him do this work?

I had intended . . .

    I had made preparations . . .

        But God . . .

What do you do with the "but God" moments in life? When God interrupts your good plans, how do you respond?

The man who lost his wife has not responded well. At this writing he indwells a fog bank of anger and bitterness. The young couple is coping better. They stay active in church and prayerful about a child. And Willem? Now that's a story. But before I share it, what about David? When God changed David's plans, how did he reply? (You'll like this.)

David faced the behemoth of disappointment with "yet God." David trusted.

He followed the "but God" with a "yet God."

Yet, the LORD, the God of Israel, chose me from all the house of my father to be king over Israel forever. For He has chosen Judah to be a leader; and in the house of Judah, my father's house, and among the sons of my father He took pleasure in me to make me king over all Israel. (1 Chron. 28:4 NASB)

Reduce the paragraph to a phrase, and it reads, "Who am I to complain? David had gone from runt to royalty, from herding sheep to leading armies, from sleeping in the pasture to living in the palace. When you are given an ice cream sundae, you don't complain over a missing cherry.

David faced the behemoth of disappointment with "yet God." David trusted.

So did Willem. Initially, he was hurt and angry. He lingered in the small village, not knowing where to turn. But one afternoon he noticed an old miner bending beneath an enormous weight of coal. Caught by the poignancy of the moment, Willem began to sketch the weary figure. His first attempt was crude, but then he tried again. He didn't know it, but at that very moment, Willem discovered his true calling.

Not the robe of clergy, but the frock of an artist.

Not the pulpit of a pastor, but the palette of a painter.

Not the ministry of words, but of images. The young man the leader would not accept became an artist the world could not resist: Vincent Willem van Gogh.[1]

His "but God" became a "yet God."

Who's to say yours won't become the same?

19

TAKE GOLIATH DOWN!

He vies for the bedside position, hoping to be the first voice you hear. He covets your waking thoughts, those early, pillow-born emotions. He awakes you with words of worry, stirs you with thoughts of stress. If you dread the day before you begin your day, mark it down: your giant has been by your bed.

And he's just getting warmed up. He breathes down your neck as you eat your breakfast, whispers in your ear as you walk out the door, shadows your steps, and sticks to your hip. He checks your calendar, reads your mail, and talks more trash than players in an inner-city basketball league.

"You ain't got what it takes."

"You come from a long line of losers."

"Fold your cards and leave the table. You've been dealt a bad hand."

He's your giant, your Goliath. Given half a chance, he'll turn your day into his Valley of Elah, taunting, teasing, boasting, and echoing claims from one hillside to the other. Remember how Goliath misbehaved? "For forty days, twice a day, morning and evening, the Philistine giant strutted in front of the Israelite army" (1 Sam. 17:16 NLT).

Goliaths still roam our world. Debt. Disaster. Dialysis. Danger. Deceit. Disease. Depression. Super-size challenges still swagger and strut, still pilfer sleep and embezzle peace and liposuction joy. But they can't dominate you. You know how to deal with them. You face giants by facing God first.

> *Focus on giants—you stumble.*
> *Focus on God—your giants tumble.*

You know what David knew, and you do what David did. You pick up five stones, and you make five decisions. Ever wonder why David took five stones into battle? Why not two or twenty? Rereading his story reveals five answers. Use your five fingers to remind you of the five stones you need to face down your Goliath. Let your thumb remind you of . . .

1. THE STONE OF THE PAST

Goliath jogged David's memory. Elah was a déjà vu. While everyone else quivered, David remembered. God had given him strength to wrestle a lion and strong-arm a bear. Wouldn't he do the same with the giant?

> David said to Saul, "Your servant used to keep his father's sheep, and when a lion or a bear came and took a lamb out of the flock, I went out after it and struck it, and delivered the lamb from its mouth; and when it arose against me, I caught it by its beard, and struck and killed it. Your servant has killed both lion and bear; and this uncircumcised Philistine will be like one of them, seeing he has defied the armies of the living God." (17:34–36)

A good memory makes heroes. A bad memory makes wimps. Amnesia made a wimp out of me last week. My Goliath awoke me at 4:00 a.m. with a woeful list of worries. Our church was attempting to raise money for a youth building, more money than we had ever raised in one effort.

Write today's worries in sand. Chisel yesterday's victories in stone.

The giant awoke me with ridicule. *You guys are crazy. You'll never collect that much money.* I couldn't argue. *The economy is down. People are stressed. We may not raise enough to buy one brick.* Goliath had me running for the trees.

But then I remembered David, the nine-to-two odds, the story of the lion and the bear. So I decided to do what David did: gaze at God's victories. I climbed out of bed, walked into the living room, turned on the lamp, pulled out my journal, and began making a list of lion- and bear-size conquests.

In the five previous years, God had prompted

- a businessman to donate several acres of land to the church;
- another church to buy our old building; and
- members to give above the needs, enabling the church to be 80 percent debt free.

God has done this before, I whispered. A lion's head hangs in the church foyer, and a bear rug rests on the sanctuary floor. About this time I heard a thud. Right there in the living room! I turned around just in time to see Goliath's eyes cross and knees buckle and body fall face-first on the carpet. I stood and placed a foot on his back and chuckled, *Take that, big boy.*[1]

"Remember His marvelous works which He has done" (1 Chron. 16:12). Catalog God's successes. Keep a list of his world records. Has he not walked you through high waters? Proven to be faithful? Have you not known his provision? How many nights have you gone to bed hungry? Mornings awakened in the cold? He has made roadkill out of your enemies. Write today's worries in sand. Chisel yesterday's victories in stone. Pick up the stone of the past. Then select . . .

2. THE STONE OF PRAYER

Note the valley between your thumb and finger. To pass from one to the next you must go through it. Let it remind you of David's descent. Before going high, David went low; before ascending to fight, David descended to prepare. Don't face your giant without first doing the same. Dedicate time to prayer. Paul, the apostle, wrote, "Prayer is essential in this ongoing warfare. Pray hard and long" (Eph. 6:18 msg).

---

*Peace is promised to the one who
fixes thoughts and desires on the king.*

Prayer spawned David's successes. His Brook Besor wisdom grew out of the moment he "strengthened himself in the Lord his God" (1 Sam. 30:6). When Saul's soldiers tried to capture him, David turned toward God: "You have been my defense and refuge in the day of my trouble" (Ps. 59:16).

How do you survive a fugitive life in the caves? David did with prayers like this one: "Be good to me, God—and now! I've run to you for dear life. I'm hiding out under your wings until the hurricane blows over. I call out to High God, the God who holds me together" (Ps. 57:1–2 msg).

When David soaked his mind in God, he stood. When he didn't, he flopped. You think he spent much time in prayer the evening he seduced Bathsheba? Did he write a psalm the day he murdered Uriah? Doubtful.

Mark well this promise: "[God] will keep in perfect peace all who trust in [God], whose thoughts are fixed on [God]" (Isa. 26:3 nlt). God promises not just peace but perfect peace. Undiluted, unspotted, unhindered peace. To whom? To those whose minds are "fixed" on God. Forget occasional glances. Dismiss random ponderings. Peace is promised to the one who fixes thoughts and desires on the king.

Invite God's help. Pick up the stone of prayer. And don't neglect . . .

3. THE STONE OF PRIORITY

Let your tallest finger remind you of your highest priority: God's reputation. David jealously guarded it. No one was going to defame his Lord. David fought so that "all the earth may know that there is a God in Israel. Then all this assembly shall know that the Lord does not save with sword and spear; for the battle is the Lord's" (1 Sam. 17:46–47).

See your struggle as God's canvas.
On it he will paint his multicolored supremacy.

David saw Goliath as a chance for God to show off! Did David know he would exit the battle alive? No. But he was willing to give his life for the reputation of God.

What if you saw your giant in the same manner? Rather than begrudge him, welcome him. Your cancer is God's chance to flex his healing muscles. Your sin is God's opportunity to showcase grace. Your struggling marriage can billboard God's power. See your struggle as God's canvas. On it he will paint his multicolored supremacy. Announce God's name and then reach for . . .

4. THE STONE OF PASSION

As Goliath moved closer to attack, David quickly ran out to meet him. Reaching into his shepherd's bag and taking out a stone, he hurled it from his sling and hit the Philistine in the forehead. The stone sank in, and Goliath stumbled and fell face downward to the ground. (17:48–49 NLT)

David ran, not away from, but toward his giant. On one side of the battlefield, Saul and his cowardly army gulped. On the other, Goliath and his skull-splitters scoffed. In the middle, the shepherd boy ran on his spindly legs. Who bet on David? Who put money on the kid from Bethlehem? Not the Philistines. Not the Hebrews. Not David's siblings or David's king. But God did.

David lobotomized the giant because he emphasized the Lord.

And since God did, and since David knew God did, the skinny runt became a blur of pumping knees and a swirling sling. He ran toward his giant.

Do the same! What good has problem-pondering gotten you? You've stared so long you can number the hairs on Goliath's chest. Has it helped?

No. Listing hurts won't heal them. Itemizing problems won't solve them. Categorizing rejections won't remove them. David lobotomized the giant because he emphasized the Lord. Let your ring finger remind you to take up the stone of passion.

One more stone, and finger, remains:

5. THE STONE OF PERSISTENCE

David didn't think one rock would do. He knew Goliath had four behemoth relatives. "Ishbi-benob was a descendant of the giants; his bronze spearhead weighed more than seven pounds" (2 Sam. 21:16 NLT). Saph made the list, described as "another descendant of the giants" (v. 18 NLT). Then there was "the brother of Goliath of Gath. The handle of his spear was as thick as a weaver's beam!" (v. 19 NLT).

Never give up.

These three seem harmless compared to King Kong.

> There was a giant there [Gath] with six fingers on his hands and six toes on his feet—twenty-four fingers and toes! He was another of those descended from Rapha. . . .
>
> These four were descended from Rapha in Gath. (vv. 20, 22 MSG)

Why did David quarry a quintet of stones? Could it be because Goliath had four relatives the size of Tyrannosaurus rex? For all David knew, they'd come running over the hill to defend their kin. David was ready to empty the chamber if that's what it took.

Imitate him. Never give up. One prayer might not be enough. One apology might not do it. One day or month of resolve might not suffice. You may get knocked down a time or two . . . but don't quit. Keep loading the rocks. Keep swinging the sling.

David took five stones. He made five decisions. Do likewise. Past. Prayer. Priority. Passion. And persistence.

Next time Goliath wakes you up, reach for a stone. Odds are, he'll be out of the room before you can load your sling.

Afterword

What Began in Bethlehem

His story started in a sheep pasture. Woolly heads witnessed his early days. Quiet fields welcomed his childish eyes. Before people heeded his message, sheep turned at his cry. Queue up the billions of creatures that have heard his voice, and grass-grazers claim a place near the front.

His story began in a pasture.

A Bethlehem pasture. Such a small hamlet sleeping on the gentle slopes. The home of shepherds. The land of figs, olives, and vines. Not lush, but sufficient. Not known to the world but known to God, who, for his reasons, chose Bethlehem as the incubator of this chosen child.

Chosen, indeed. Chosen by God. Anointed from on high, set apart by heaven. The prophet declared the call. The family heard it.

The lad of the sheep would be a shepherd of souls. Bethlehem's boy would be Israel's king.

But not before he became the target of hell.

The road out of Bethlehem was steep and dangerous. It led him through a lizard-laced desert, an angry Jerusalem, conflict, and peril. Leaders resolved to kill him. His people sought to stone him. His own family chose to mock him.

Some people lifted him up him as king; others cast him down. Jerusalem gates saw him enter as a sovereign and leave like a fugitive. He eventually died a lonely death in the Hebrew capital.

But he is far from dead.

His words still speak. His legacy still lives. Love or hate him, society keeps turning to him, reading his thoughts, pondering his deeds, imagining his face. Scripture gives only scant sentences about his looks, so sculptors and artists have filled galleries with their speculations. Michelangelo. Rembrandt. Da Vinci. Canvas. Stone. Painting. Sculpting.

And books. Books! More pages have been devoted to Bethlehem's prodigy than any other figure in history. We can't stop talking about him. Sand has filled his Judean footprints thousands of times over thousands of years—but still we gather to reflect on his life.

You know whom I'm describing.

You do, don't you? The pasture. The anointing. The childhood call. The lifelong enemies. Wilderness. Jerusalem. Judea. The lonely death. The endless legacy. Who is this boy from Bethlehem?

David, of course.

Or Jesus, perhaps.

Or . . . both?

What Began in Bethlehem

List a dozen facts, and in each describe twin traits of David and Jesus. Amazing. Even more so is the fact that we can do the same with your life. Read these truths and tell me, who am I describing? Jesus . . . or you?

> Born to a mother.
> Acquainted with physical pain.
> Enjoys a good party.
> Rejected by friends.
> Unfairly accused.
> Loves stories.
> Reluctantly pays taxes.
> Sings.
> Turned off by greedy religion.
> Feels sorry for the lonely.
> Unappreciated by siblings.
> Stands up for the underdog.
> Kept awake at night by concerns.
> Known to doze off in the midst of trips.
> Accused of being too rowdy.
> Afraid of death.

You?

Jesus?

Both?

Seems you, like David, have much in common with Jesus.

Big deal? I think so. Jesus understands you. He understands small-town anonymity and big-city pressure. He's walked pastures of sheep and palaces of kings. He's faced hunger, sorrow, and death and wants to face them with you. Jesus "understands our weaknesses, for he faced all of the same temptations we do, yet he did not sin. So let us come boldly to the throne of our gracious God. There we will receive his mercy, and we will find grace to help us when we need it" (Heb. 4:15–16 NLT).

He became one of us. And he did so to redeem all of us.

The stories of David and Jesus share many names: Bethlehem, Judea, Jerusalem. The Mount of Olives. The Dead Sea. En Gedi. While their stories are similar, don't for a second think they are identical.

He became one of us . . . to redeem all of us.

Jesus had no Bathsheba collapse, Uriah murder, or adultery cover-up. Jesus never pillaged a village, camped with the enemy, or neglected a child. No one accused the fairest son of Bethlehem of polygamy, brutality, or adultery. In fact, no one successfully accused Jesus of anything.

They tried. My, how they tried. But when accusers called him a son of Satan, Jesus asked for their proof. "Can any one of you convict me of a single misleading word, a single sinful act?" (John 8:46 MSG). No one could. Disciples traveled with him. Enemies scrutinized him. Admirers studied him. But no one could convict him of sin.

No one spotted him in the wrong place, heard him say the wrong words, or saw him respond the wrong way. Peter, three years Jesus's companion, said, "He never did one thing wrong. Not once said anything amiss" (1 Pet. 2:22 MSG). Pilate was the head of the Roman version of the CIA, yet when he tried to find fault in Jesus, he failed (John 18:38). Even the demons called Jesus "the Holy One of God" (Luke 4:34 NIV).

Jesus never missed the mark.

Equally amazing, he never distances himself from those who do.

Just read the first verse of Matthew's gospel. Jesus knew David's ways. He witnessed the adultery, winced at the murders, and grieved at the dishonesty. But David's failures didn't change Jesus's relation to David. The initial verse of the first chapter of the first gospel calls Christ "the son of David" (Matt. 1:1 KJV). The title contains no disclaimers, explanations, or asterisks. I'd have added a footnote: "This connection in no way offers tacit approval to David's behavior." No such words appear. David blew it. Jesus knew it. But he claimed David anyway.

He did for David what my father did for my brother and me.

Back in our elementary school days, my brother received a BB gun for Christmas. We immediately set up a firing range in the backyard and spent the afternoon shooting at an archery target. Growing bored with the ease of hitting the circle, my brother sent me to fetch a hand mirror. He placed the gun backward on his shoulder, spotted the archery bull's-eye in the mirror, and did his best Buffalo Bill imitation. But he missed the target. He also missed the storehouse behind the target and the fence behind the storehouse. We had no idea where the BB pellet flew. Our neighbor across the alley knew, however. He soon appeared at the back fence, asking who had shot the BB gun and who was going to pay for his sliding-glass door.

At this point I disowned my brother. I changed my last name and claimed to be a holiday visitor from Canada. My father was more noble than I. Hearing the noise, he appeared in the backyard, freshly rousted from his Christmas Day nap, and talked with the neighbor.

Among his words were these:

"Yes, they are my children."

"Yes, I'll pay for their mistakes."

Christ says the same about you. He knows you miss the target. He knows you can't pay for your mistakes. But he can. "God sent Jesus to take the punishment for our sins" (Rom. 3:25 NLT).

Since he was sinless, he could.

Since he loves you, he did. "This is real love. It is not that we loved God, but that he loved us and sent his Son as a sacrifice to take away our sins" (1 John 4:10 NLT).

He calls you brother; he calls you sister.
The question is, do you call him Savior?

He became one of us to redeem all of us. "Jesus, who makes people holy, and those who are made holy are from the same family. So he is not ashamed to call them his brothers and sisters" (Heb. 2:11 NCV).

He wasn't ashamed of David. He isn't ashamed of you. He calls you brother; he calls you sister. The question is, do you call him Savior?

Take a moment to answer this question. Perhaps you never have. Perhaps you never knew how much Christ loves you. Now you do. Jesus didn't disown David. He won't disown you. He simply awaits your invitation. One word from you, and God will do again what he did with David and millions like him: he'll claim you, save you, and use you. Any words will do, but these seem appropriate:

Jesus, my Savior and Giant-killer, I trust you with my heart and give you my life. I ask for mercy, strength, and eternal life. Amen.

Pray such words with an honest heart, and be assured of this: your greatest Goliath has fallen. Your failures are flushed and death defanged. The power that made pygmies out of David's giants has done the same with yours.

You can face your giants. Why? Because you faced God first.

Study Guide

Written by Steve Halliday

1

Facing Your Giants

Reconnaissance

1. You know Goliath. You recognize his walk and wince at his talk. You've seen your Godzilla. The question is, is he all you see? You know his voice—but is it all you hear?
   A. What Goliaths have you confronted in the past?
   B. How does your Goliath block your vision of God and make it harder to hear from the Lord?

2. David majors in God. He sees the giant, mind you; he just sees God more so.
   A. What do you think it means to major in God?
   B. How does majoring in God help to shrink the Goliaths of your life?

3. David's life has little to offer the unstained saint. Straight-A souls find David's story disappointing. The rest of us find it

reassuring. We ride the same roller coaster. We alternate
between swan dives and belly flops, soufflés and burnt toast.

    A. In what arenas of life are you most likely to do swan
dives and to make soufflés? In what arenas of life are
you most likely to do belly flops and to burn toast?

    B. Do you find David's story reassuring? Why or why not?

4. God-thoughts outnumber Goliath-thoughts nine to two. How
does this ratio compare with yours? Do you ponder God's
grace four times as much as you ponder your guilt? Is your
list of blessings four times as long as your list of complaints?
Is your mental file of hope four times as thick as your mental
file of dread? Are you four times as likely to describe the
strength of God as you are the demands of your day?

    A. How would you answer each of Max's questions above?

    B. How could you begin to increase your God-thoughts
and decrease your Goliath-thoughts?

5. Focus on giants—you stumble. Focus on God—your giants
tumble.

    A. When you focus on your giants, what kind of stumbles
do you tend to take?

    B. When you focus on God, what kind of tumbles do your
giants tend to take?

Marching Orders

1. Read 1 Samuel 17:1–54.

    A. How did David's perspective differ from his country-
men's perspective?

    B. What reason does David give for his confidence in a
fight against Goliath (vv. 34–37)?

    C. What do verses 45–47 reveal about the man after God's
own heart?

2. Read Isaiah 51:12–15.
    A. Why does the Lord say we should not fear mere mortals?
    B. What happens when we forget our Creator?
    C. What kind of plans does God have for us?

3. Read Hebrews 12:1–3.
    A. In your own experience, whose lives encourage your faith? Why?
    B. Why should we fix our eyes on Jesus? How is he described?
    C. What is the result of fixing our eyes on him in this way?

Battle Lines

What is the biggest problem you face right now? What Goliath is staring you in the face, taunting you and defying God to rescue you? Set aside an hour in which you focus on God—on his power and his wisdom and his glory—and in which you concentrate your prayers for help on this problem. Watch God make the fast a turning point in this battle!

2

SILENT PHONES

Reconnaissance

1. You know the feeling. The phone didn't ring for you either. . . . When you applied for the job or for the club, tried to make up or to get help . . . the call never came. You know the pain of a no call. We all do.

A. Describe the last time the phone didn't ring for you. What happened?

B. Why is it so painful when the call doesn't come?

2. The Hebrew word for "youngest son" is *haqqaton*. It implies more than age; it suggests rank. The *haqqaton* was more than the youngest brother; he was the *little* brother—the runt, the hobbit, the "bay-ay-ay-bee."

A. In what ways have you been the *haqqaton* of some group or organization that was important to you?

B. What is the hardest thing about being the runt of the litter?

3. Oh, the Goliath of exclusion. Are you sick of him? Then it's time to quit staring at him. Who cares what he, or they, think? What matters is what your Maker thinks.

A. Why is it so hard to stop staring at the Goliath of exclusion?

B. What do you think your Maker thinks of you—right now, today, at this very moment?

4. God saw what no one else saw: a God-seeking heart. David, for all his foibles, sought God like a lark seeks sunrise. He took after God's heart, because he stayed after God's heart. In the end, that's all God wanted or needed . . . wants or needs.

A. What do you think it means to seek God's heart?

B. Do you have a God-seeking heart? How does a God-hungry heart direct your days?

5. The story of young David assures us of this: your Father knows your heart, and because he does, he has a place reserved just for you.

   A. Does it comfort you or alarm you that God knows your heart? Explain.

   B. Do you think God has a place reserved just for you? Why or why not?

Marching Orders

1. Read 1 Samuel 15–16 and 1 Chronicles 10:13–14.
   - A. Why did the Lord reject Saul as king?
   - B. How did Samuel's fear of Saul threaten God's will?
   - C. What was the result of Saul's disobedience?

2. Read 1 Samuel 13:14 and Acts 13:22.
   - A. According to 1 Samuel 13:14, what trait or characteristic was God looking for in the person who would lead his people?
   - B. According to Acts 13:22, how would this sought-after characteristic display itself in David's life?
   - C. Is this characteristic found in your life? Does your behavior confirm or deny this characteristic?

3. Read 2 Chronicles 16:9a.
   - A. For whom do the Lord's eyes constantly scan the planet?
   - B. Why does the Lord search for such people?
   - C. How can you increasingly become this sort of person?

Battle Lines

One of the best ways to become a person after God's own heart is to spend time around men and women after God's own heart. Identify two to three mature believers who you believe have a close walk with Christ, and ask to interview them. Find out what makes them tick, how they nurture their relationship with God, and what they do when they grow discouraged.

3

RAGING SAULS

Reconnaissance

1. What ogres roam your world? Controlling moms. Coaches from the school of Stalin. The pit-bull math teacher. The self-appointed cubicle commandant.

   A. How would you answer Max's question above?

   B. When your ogres confront you, how do you normally react?

2. How does God respond in such cases? Nuke the nemesis? We may want him to. He's been known to extract a few Herods and Pharaohs. How he will treat yours, I can't say. But how he will treat you, I can. He will send you a Jonathan.

   A. Why do you think God responds in such different ways to the many nemeses that cause such trouble in our world?

   B. Who is the Jonathan that God sent you? Describe him or her.

3. You long for one true friend? You have one. And because you do, you have a choice. You can focus on your Saul or your Jonathan, ponder the malice of your monster or the kindness of your Christ.

   A. Where do you tend to place your focus when a Saul or a monster confronts you?

   B. How can you get better at choosing to focus on the kindness of your Christ? What practical steps could you take?

4. Linger too long in the stench of your hurt, and you'll smell like the toxin you despise.
   A. Of the hurts you've suffered, which has the most power to keep you trapped?
   B. Why does dwelling on a terrible hurt make you smell like the toxin you despise?

5. Wander freely and daily through the gallery of God's goodness. Catalog his kindnesses. Everything from sunsets to salvation—look at what you have. Your Saul took much, but Christ gave you more! Let Jesus be the friend you need.
   A. Take a pen and a sheet of paper, and catalog the kindnesses that God has lavished on you just this week.
   B. In what ways has Christ given you more than your Saul has taken?

Marching Orders

1. Read 1 Samuel 18:6–29.
   A. What first made Saul angry with David? Why did this make him angry?
   B. What made Saul afraid of David (v. 12)?
   C. What actions were caused by Saul's jealousy?

2. Read 1 Samuel 18:1–4; 20:1–42; 23:16.
   A. How would you describe David's friendship with Jonathan?
   B. Who risked more, David or Jonathan, by this friendship?
   C. What is perhaps the most important element of a deep friendship as shown by 1 Samuel 23:16? What is meant by "strengthened his hand in God"?

3. Read 2 Timothy 4:16–18.
   A. Which of Paul's friends stood with him at the end of his life?
   B. Who did stand with Paul?
   C. How did this friendship give Paul great strength and encouragement?

Battle Lines
We are told that Jonathan "strengthened [David's] hand in God." One of the best ways to grow spiritually is to help someone else grow spiritually. Who do you know that might need some encouragement right now? Take the initiative, and do what you can to "strengthen _____'s hand in God." Make sure you do this authentically, genuinely, and sensitively.

4

DESPERATE DAYS

Reconnaissance
1. David's faith is wavering. Not too long ago the shepherd's sling was all he needed. Now the one who refused the armor and sword of Saul requests a weapon from the priest. What has happened to our hero? Simple. He's lost his God-focus.
   A. What do you think caused David to lose his God-focus?
   B. What usually prompts you to lose your God-focus?

2. Bread and blades. Food and equipment. The church exists to provide both.

Study Guide

    A. How does your church supply "bread" (food) and "blades" (equipment) to those who need them?

    B. What part do you play in this supply line?

3. Jesus calls the church to lean in the direction of compassion.

    A. Why is compassion so important to Jesus?

    B. How do you tend to show others the compassion of Jesus?

4. At the end of the sanctuary day, the question is not how many laws were broken but rather, how many desperate Davids were nourished and equipped? Ahimelech teaches the church to pursue the spirit of the law more than its letter.

    A. Do you find it easier to pursue the spirit of the law or its letter? Explain.

    B. What tends to happen when you pursue the spirit of the law rather than the letter of the law?

5. David stumbles in this story. Desperate souls always do. But at least he stumbles into the right place—into God's sanctuary, where God meets and ministers to hopeless hearts.

    A. In the past year, how has God ministered to you after a stumble?

    B. Who in your life needs to be ministered to after a stumble?

Marching Orders

1. Read 1 Samuel 21:1–9.

    A. Why do you think David lied to the priest?

    B. Why did David want Goliath's sword?

    C. Does taking a sword necessarily imply a lack of faith? Explain.

2. Read Romans 8:38–39.
   A. What confidence does Paul express in this passage?
   B. How does such confidence help someone to face life's difficulties?
   C. Do you have this confidence? Why or why not?

3. Read John 20:19–22.
   A. How does Jesus respond to the fear of his disciples?
   B. What mission did Jesus give to his disciples?
   C. What power did Jesus give his disciples to accomplish their mission?

Battle Lines

As a member of Christ's church, it is your privilege to provide others with food and equipment. Who in your church could use some basic necessities? Reach out to someone in need this week.

5

DRY SEASONS

Reconnaissance

1. Wilderness begins with disconnections. It continues with deceit.
   A. What has happened in your life when you disconnected from important relationships?
   B. Why does deceit so often follow personal disconnections? What do disconnection and deceit lead to?

2. Has your Saul cut you off from the position you had and the people you love? In an effort to land on your feet, have you stretched the truth? Distorted the facts? Are you seeking refuge in Gath? Under normal circumstances you would

never go there. But these aren't normal circumstances, so you loiter in the breeding ground of giants.

   A. How would you answer Max's questions above?

   B. What is Gath for you? What would cause you to loiter there?

3. Make God your refuge. Not your job, your spouse, your reputation, or your retirement account. Make God your refuge. Let him, not Saul, encircle you. Let him be the ceiling that breaks the sunshine, the walls that stop the wind, the foundation on which you stand.

   A. How do you make God your refuge?

   B. What needs to change in your life if you are to make God your refuge?

4. "You'll never know that Jesus is all you need until Jesus is all you have."

   A. Do you agree with the statement above? Why or why not?

   B. Has there ever been a time in your life when you had nothing but Jesus? If so, describe it.

5. Are you in the wilderness? Crawl into God the way a fugitive would a cave. Find refuge in God's presence and comfort in his people. Those are your keys for wilderness survival.

   A. Describe a time when you sought refuge in God's presence.

   B. How have God's people given you comfort? How have you, as one of God's people, given comfort to others?

Marching Orders

1. Read 1 Samuel 21:10–22:2.

   A. What made David afraid?

    B. How did David act because of his fear?

    C. Did his actions hurt him or help him? Explain.

2. Read Psalm 57:1–3.

    A. Where does David turn for help from his enemies?

    B. What does "refuge" mean for David in this psalm?

    C. What answer does David expect to receive from God? Why does he expect this answer?

3. Read 1 Corinthians 1:26–31.

    A. How does Paul characterize the members of the church? Why is this significant?

    B. Why does God choose the ones he chooses? What does he hope to accomplish?

    C. According to this passage, what should be the perspective of a believer in Christ?

Battle Lines

Those who most need comfort often won't risk asking for it. Put your antennae up, and look around for someone who seems to feel disconnected and alone. Invite that person to go to lunch or to take a walk with you. Don't go prepared with a talk, but just "be there" for him or her—and ask God to use your efforts to help that person find refuge in him.

6

GRIEF-GIVERS

Reconnaissance

1. Think about the purveyors of pain in your life. It's one thing to give grace to friends, but to give grace to those who give you grief? Could you?

A. Who are the purveyors of pain in your life? What would it take for you to give grace to them? What do you think it would look like?

B. How do you avoid the natural human tendency to give grief to those who give grief to you? How could you make it a habit to give these people grace rather than grief?

2. Vengeance fixes your attention at life's ugliest moments. Score-settling freezes your stare at cruel events in your past. Is this where you want to look? Will rehearsing and reliving your hurts make you a better person? By no means. It will destroy you.

A. Think of someone you know whom you would describe as a vengeful, score-settling person. How happy do you think that person is? Explain.

B. Why do vengeance and a life of retribution destroy the one who engages in such behavior?

3. Your enemies still figure into God's plan. Their pulse is proof: God hasn't given up on them. They may be out of God's will, but not out of his reach. You honor God when you see them, not as his failures, but as his projects.

A. How does it help you to think of your enemies as God's projects?

B. Use your imagination for a moment: how could God use your enemies to benefit you and bring him glory?

4. Forgiveness is not excusing. Nor is forgiveness pretending. David didn't gloss over or sidestep Saul's sin. He addressed it directly. He didn't avoid the issue, but he did avoid Saul.

A. Is it compatible to forgive someone and still purposefully avoid him or her? Explain.

B. If forgiveness is not excusing or pretending, what is it? What does it look like? Whom do you most need to forgive right now?

5. Dare we ask God for grace when we refuse to give it? This is a huge issue in Scripture. Jesus was tough on sinners who refused to forgive other sinners.
   A. In God's eyes, is your sin any less sinful than that of someone who hurt you? Explain.
   B. Why do you think Jesus was so tough on sinners who refused to forgive other sinners? What might Jesus say to you personally on this subject?

Marching Orders
1. Read 1 Samuel 24, 26.
   A. How did David's men twist a prophecy to encourage David to do evil (24:4)?
   B. Why did David give Saul such great esteem (24:5–7)? Who was David really honoring by his conduct?
   C. Into whose hands did David commit both his and Saul's destiny (26:10–11)?

2. Read Romans 12:14–21.
   A. How are believers in Christ supposed to treat their enemies?
   B. Why are believers forbidden from taking revenge (v. 19)?
   C. Instead of taking revenge, what strategy does God give his children (vv. 20–21)?

3. Read Colossians 3:13.
   A. What does it mean to bear with each other?
   B. Why are believers to forgive those who hurt them?

   C. Why did the Lord forgive you? What aspects of the Lord's forgiveness can you imitate?

Battle Lines

Is there someone you've been unable to forgive in the past? Spend some time prayerfully determining to forgive that person. If possible, attempt a reconciliation. Do not let bitterness acidize your soul.

7

BARBARIC BEHAVIOR

Reconnaissance

1. Their goodness proves contagious, and Gordon contracts a case. He begins to treat the sick and share his rations. He even gives away his few belongings. Other soldiers do likewise. Over time, the tone of the camp softens and brightens.

   A. Describe a time you saw the good influence of one person change the atmosphere of a group or organization.

   B. What specific environment could you reshape by your good influence?

2. Do personal possessive pronouns dominate the language of your circle? *My* career, *my* dreams, *my* stuff. I want things to go *my* way on *my* schedule. If so, you know how savage this giant can be.

   A. Think back over your day. How much of your time was consumed by thoughts of yourself?

   B. What's the biggest problem with a sustained self-focus to the exclusion of all else?

3. Abigail's gentleness reversed a river of anger. Humility has such power. Apologies can disarm arguments. Contrition can defuse rage. Olive branches do more good than battle-axes ever will.

    A. Describe the gentlest person you ever knew. What kind of influence did this person have on others?

    B. Is humility a struggle for you? Why or why not?

4. Abigail placed herself between David and Nabal. Jesus placed himself between God and us. Abigail volunteered to be punished for Nabal's sins. Jesus allowed heaven to punish him for yours and mine. Abigail turned away the anger of David. Didn't Christ shield you from God's?

    A. What do you think motivated Abigail to act as she did?

    B. Did Christ shield you from the wrath of God? Explain.

5. One prisoner can change a camp. One Abigail can save a family. Be the beauty amidst your beasts and see what happens.

    A. How could you be the beauty that brings peace to a tense or combative situation?

    B. What would you hope to accomplish?

Marching Orders

1. Read 1 Samuel 25.

    A. How did Abigail's servant characterize the treatment he and his friends had received from David and his men (vv. 14–16)?

    B. What lie did David tell himself as he prepared to take vengeance on Nabal (vv. 21–22)?

    C. Who kept David from taking vengeance, according to Abigail (v. 26)? Why is this significant?

2. Read Proverbs 15:1.
   A. Which half of this verse did Nabal demonstrate?
   B. Which half of this verse did Abigail demonstrate?
   C. Which half of this verse do you normally demonstrate?

3. Read Philippians 4:5.
   A. What trait does this verse urge believers to display? To whom is this trait to be displayed?
   B. What unexpected thought is connected to this command? How do you think it's connected in thought?
   C. What do you think it means to be gentle?

Battle Lines

Think of a person whom you have injured, insulted, or alienated. Ask God to give you the grace and the humility to approach this person and ask for forgiveness. It may be tough, but pray that the Lord will bring peace and healing to the situation.

8

SLUMP GUNS

Reconnaissance

1. No hope and, most of all, no God. David focuses on Saul. He hangs Saul's poster on his wall and replays his voice messages. David immerses himself in his fear until his fear takes over: "I will be destroyed."
   A. Why do "no hope" and "no God" often go together?
   B. What most often causes you to think, *I will be destroyed*?

2. Hiding out with the enemy brings temporary relief. Doesn't it always? Stop resisting alcohol, and you'll laugh—for a

while. Move out on your spouse, and you'll relax—for a time. Indulge in the porn, and you'll be entertained—for a season. But then talons of temptation sink in. Waves of guilt crash in. The loneliness of breaking up rushes in.

    A. In what ways do you sometimes hide out with the enemy? What do you hope to gain from this?

    B. Why does hiding out with the enemy not work ultimately?

3. Stop talking to yourself. Talk to Christ, who invites, "Are you tired? Worn out? Burned out on religion? Come to me. Get away with me and you'll recover your life. I'll show you how to take a real rest" (Matt. 11:28 MSG).

    A. What kind of tapes play over and over in your head? What kind of unproductive things do you keep telling yourself?

    B. Have you ever experienced the rest of Jesus? If so, describe it. If not, what prevents you from seeking it?

4. Be quick to pray, seek healthy counsel, and don't give up.

    A. What is the relationship between regular prayer and the ability to endure?

    B. Whom can you go to for healthy counsel?

5. Don't be fooled by the fog of the slump. The finish may be only strokes away. God may be, at this moment, lifting his hand to signal Gabriel to grab the trumpet. Angels may be assembling, saints gathering, demons trembling. Stay at it! Stay in the water. Stay in the race. Stay in the fight. Give grace, one more time. Be generous, one more time. Teach one more class, encourage one more soul, swim one more stroke.

    A. What good thing or task are you most tempted to give up on right now?

B. Describe an instance where someone you know finished strong despite the obstacles. What impact did that example have on you?

Marching Orders

1. Read 1 Samuel 27.
   A. In what way was David's whole strategy to escape Saul based on a lie (v. 1)?
   B. How did David's whole strategy for staying in Philistia depend on a stream of lies (vv. 8–11)?
   C. Why are lies never a good basis for building a sound future?

2. Read Proverbs 14:12.
   A. How did David's Philistine stopover illustrate the truth of this verse?
   B. If God's ways are always better than ours, then why do we so often choose our own ways?
   C. How can you make sure that your life doesn't illustrate the truth of this verse?

3. Read Matthew 11:28.
   A. What is the promise described in this verse?
   B. To whom is the promise addressed?
   C. What must one do to take advantage of the promise given in this verse?

Battle Lines

Designate this "accentuate the positive" week. Consciously give positive comments to those you come into contact with, especially those who may not be expecting it: a grocery clerk, a neighbor, the mailman, a waiter. At the end of the week, note what happened—both to you and to them.

Study Guide

9

PLOPPING POINTS

Reconnaissance

1. Support systems don't always support. Friends aren't always friendly. Pastors can wander off base and churches get out of touch. When no one can help, we have to do what David does here. He turns toward God.

   A. Describe a time when one of your support systems failed you. How did you respond? Where did you turn?

   B. In what area of your life do you most need to turn to God?

2. What do we do with the Brook Besor people? Berate them? Shame them? Give them a rest but measure the minutes? Or do we do what David did? David let them stay.

   A. What do you tend to do with Brook Besor people?

   B. When was the last time you were a Brook Besor person? Did a David let you stay? Explain.

3. David did many mighty deeds in his life. He did many foolish deeds in his life. But perhaps the noblest was this rarely discussed deed: he honored the tired soldiers at Brook Besor.

   A. Why would Max say that David's noblest deed was to honor his tired soldiers at Brook Besor? Would you agree? Explain.

   B. Who are the tired soldiers in your life that you could honor as David did? In what specific ways could you honor them?

4. It's okay to rest. Jesus is your David. He fights when you cannot. He goes where you cannot. He's not angry if you sit.

A. Do you ever feel that Jesus is angry with you when you sit? Explain.

B. In what ways has Jesus fought for you when you could not? Describe a few specific instances.

Marching Orders

1. Read 1 Samuel 30:1–25.
    A. How did David make it through this terrible ordeal (v. 6)?
    B. How did God show his grace to David, despite David's misadventures in Philistine territory (vv. 18–19)?
    C. Whom did David credit with his victory (v. 23)? How does this help to explain his order about the plunder?

2. Read Mark 6:31.
    A. How would you describe the activity level of the disciples in this scene?
    B. What was Jesus's prescription for his tired disciples?
    C. How does Jesus's prescription relate to your situation?

3. Read Philemon 1:20.
    A. What was Paul requesting here?
    B. How did Paul expect to benefit if his request was granted?
    C. Whose heart can you "refresh . . . in the Lord" today? How could you do this?

Battle Lines

It really is all right to stop for a while and get some rest. So take a break! Go somewhere that feels refreshing and relaxing to you, and just hang out. Visit a garden, take a walk in the park, go for a drive—whatever helps you to recharge your batteries. Turn off your cell phone, leave work behind, and get some rest. God will be pleased.

10

UNSPEAKABLE GRIEF

Reconnaissance

1. The grave stirs such unspeakable hurt and unanswerable questions, we're tempted to turn and walk. Change the subject, avoid the issue. Work hard. Drink harder. Stay busy. Stay distant. Head north to Montana and don't look back.

   A. How do you tend to react to death, especially the death of a loved one?

   B. Why do so many of us avoid thinking about grief? What does this usually accomplish?

2. Just when you think the beast of grief is gone, you hear a song she loved or smell the cologne he wore or pass a restaurant where the two of you used to eat. The giant keeps showing up.

   A. How has sorrow returned to you without warning?

   B. When the giant of grief stalks you, how do you tend to respond? How do you deal with personal grief?

3. Understand the gravity of your loss. You didn't lose at Monopoly or misplace your keys. You can't walk away from this. At some point, within minutes or months, you need to do what David did. Face your grief.

   A. Think of the biggest loss you're dealing with at this moment. How would you describe it?

   B. What Scriptures have brought comfort to you in the heaviness of grief?

4. We spelunk life's deepest issues in the cave of sorrow. Why am I here? Where am I headed? Cemetery strolls stir hard yet vital questions.

A. What key issues of life has death forced you to grapple with?
B. With what specific questions has death left you? What answers are you still seeking?

5. So go ahead, face your grief. Give yourself time. Permit yourself tears. God understands. He knows the sorrow of a grave. He buried his son. But he also knows the joy of resurrection. And, by his power, you will too.
    A. Do you think there is a general time limit for grief? Explain.
    B. Do you look forward to the joy of resurrection? If so, why? If not, why not?

Marching Orders

1. Read 1 Samuel 31–2 Samuel 1.
    A. Why do you think God allowed Jonathan to die alongside his father, Saul?
    B. Why did David treat the young Amalekite in this story so harshly?
    C. What do you learn of David's friendship with Jonathan in this passage?

2. Read Ecclesiastes 7:3–4.
    A. What does God think about believers mourning their dead?
    B. How can mourning ever be better than laughter?
    C. What godly purpose does mourning serve?

3. Read 1 Thessalonians 4:13–18.
    A. Does verse 13 tell believers that it is inappropriate to mourn the death of their loved ones? How does it counsel believers?

    B. What promise does this text give to all believers in Christ? How does this promise give them hope?

    C. Why is it important to tell one another the truth about what will happen when Jesus returns (v. 18)?

Battle Lines

Many in our culture find it hard to grieve. We think that grieving should have a set time limit or that it should be hidden from public view. To get a better idea of what constitutes healthy grieving, consider reading a book such as *A Grief Observed* by C. S. Lewis or *Letters to a Grieving Heart* by Billy Sprague.

11

BLIND INTERSECTIONS

Reconnaissance

  1. One of life's giant-size questions is *How can I know what God wants me to do?*

    A. What do you think God has called you to do and to be? What do you believe is his overarching goal for your life?

    B. If you can't currently identify God's purpose for your life, how can you find out what his will for you really is?

  2. You have a Bible? Read it.

    A. Describe your current Bible-reading habits.

    B. How would you like to improve your comprehension of the Bible? How might you be able to make your Bible reading more interactive with the Holy Spirit of God?

  3. You have a family of faith? Consult it.

    A. How connected are you to a family of faith? Who there could serve as an effective consultant for you?

B. How often do you go to someone else for help in determining God's will for you? Why is this a wise practice?

4. You have a heart for God? Heed it.
   A. On the following scale, where would you put your heart for God?
   Icy—Frigid—Cold—Cool—Lukewarm—Warm—Hot—Blistering
   B. How could you better use your heart for God to discern God's will for you?

5. People have been known to justify stupidity based on a "feeling." "I felt God leading me to cheat on my wife . . . disregard my bills . . . lie to my boss . . . flirt with my married neighbor." Mark it down: God will not lead you to violate his Word. He will not contradict his teaching.
   A. Do you know God's Word well enough that it can keep you from making a foolish decision based on a feeling? Explain.
   B. Describe a time when the wisdom of the Bible kept you or someone you know from making a foolish decision based on a feeling.

Marching Orders
1. Read 2 Samuel 2:1–4.
   A. What specific directions did David ask for in this passage? What kind of answers did he get? What does this teach you, if anything, about prayer?
   B. What happened when David followed the direction God gave to him? Do you think this would have happened had he not followed God's guidance? Explain.
   C. What connection, if any, do you see between this passage and the principle outlined in James 4:2?

2. Read Psalm 32:8 and Proverbs 3:5–6.
   A. What does God promise in Psalm 32:8? On whom does the major responsibility for guidance fall?
   B. What is the believer's responsibility in discovering God's will, according to Proverbs 3:5? What does this look like in practical terms?
   C. What promise does Scripture give in Proverbs 3:6 regarding the discovery of God's will for a person's life? Are any exceptions given?

3. Read Philippians 2:13; 4:6; Ephesians 2:10.
   A. How does Philippians 2:13 relate to discovering God's will for your life? What encouragement does it give you?
   B. If you are anxious about discovering God's will for you, what does Philippians 4:6 encourage you to do?
   C. What further encouragement do you find in Ephesians 2:10 in regard to discovering (and doing) God's will for your life? How committed is God to this process?

Battle Lines

How effective do you think you are at discovering God's will for your life? The Bible actually says quite a lot about finding and doing God's will. Get out a concordance and look up all the references you can find to "the will of God" or "God's will." What do you discover?

12

STRONGHOLDS

Reconnaissance

1. Where does Satan have a stronghold within you? . . . "You ain't touching this flaw," he defies heaven, placing himself

squarely between God's help and your explosive temper, fragile self-image, freezer-size appetite, distrust for authority.

   A. How would you answer Max's question above?

   B. What have you tried to do to rid yourself of this stronghold?

2. Wouldn't you love God to write a *nevertheless* in your biography? Born to alcoholics, *nevertheless* she led a sober life. Dropped out of college, *nevertheless* he mastered a trade. Didn't read the Bible until retirement age, *nevertheless* he came to a deep and abiding faith.

   A. What *nevertheless* would you love for God to write into your biography?

   B. What *nevertheless* has God already written into your biography?

3. You and I fight with toothpicks; God comes with battering rams and cannons. What he did for David, he can do for us.

   A. What toothpicks have you been using to fight your battles? How well have they worked?

   B. Have you asked God to do for you what he did for David? What was his response?

4. Two types of thoughts continually vie for your attention. One says, "Yes you can." The other says, "No you can't." One says, "God will help you." The other lies, "God has left you." One speaks the language of heaven; the other deceives in the vernacular of the Jebusites. One proclaims God's strengths; the other lists your failures. One longs to build you up; the other seeks to tear you down. And here's the great news: you select the voice you hear.

   A. Which voice do you most often hear—the one that trumpets God's strengths or the one that recounts your failures?

B. How can you get better at listening to the voice that builds you up and disregarding the voice that tears you down?

Marching Orders

1. Read 2 Samuel 5:6–10.
   A. What kind of opposition did David face here? How did he handle it?
   B. What reason is given for David's military prowess (v. 10)?
   C. How can you best follow David's example to succeed against your obstacles?

2. Read 2 Corinthians 10:3–5.
   A. What kind of warfare is described in this passage? How much of this kind of battle have you seen?
   B. Who or what is the enemy, according to verse 4 (NCV)? What kind of weapons must be used in this fight? Where do these weapons get their power?
   C. What hard work is described in verse 5? Do you labor at this work? Explain.

3. Read Ephesians 1:19–20.
   A. What resources has God given you in order to succeed in the Christian life?
   B. How do you know that these resources are sufficient to overcome any opposition you may face?
   C. How can what happened long ago be a source of strength for you today?

Battle Lines

An ongoing challenge can be tough to fight alone. Approach a trusted, mature friend, and enlist his or her help in tackling this stronghold. Make it a matter of sustained prayer, and ask your friend to do the same. Keep a journal to record the progress you make in attacking this stronghold.

13

DISTANT DEITY

Reconnaissance

1. Is God a distant deity? Mothers ask, "How can the presence of God come over my children?" Fathers ponder, "How can God's presence fill my house?" Churches desire the touching, helping, healing presence of God in their midst.
    A. Do you think God is a distant deity? Explain.
    B. How would your life change if you were sure that God is not distant but very present in your everyday experiences?

2. God comes, mind you. But he comes on his own terms. He comes when commands are revered, hearts are clean, and confession is made.
    A. Do you think it is good news that God comes on his own terms? Explain.
    B. Would you say that you revere God's commands? Would you call your heart clean? Do you make it a habit to confess your sins?

3. Scripture doesn't portray David dancing at any other time. He did no death dance over Goliath. He never scooted the boot among the Philistines. He didn't inaugurate his term as king with a waltz or dedicate Jerusalem with a ballroom swirl. But when God came to town, he couldn't sit still.

    A. Why do you think David danced so energetically when the ark came to Jerusalem?

    B. Is the presence of God an occasion for dancing in your life? Explain.

4. God loves you too much to leave you alone, so he hasn't. He hasn't left you alone with your fears, your worries, your disease, or your death. So kick up your heels for joy.

    A. How does it make you feel that God has promised never to leave you alone?

    B. How can God's promise to remain with you forever give you strength to move forward *today*?

5. Uzzah's lifeless body cautions against irreverence. No awe of God leads to the death of man. God won't be cajoled, commanded, conjured up, or called down. He is a personal God who loves and heals and helps and intervenes. He doesn't respond to magic potions or clever slogans. He looks for more. He looks for reverence, obedience, and God-hungry hearts.

    A. How do you display your awe of God?

    B. What is the connection between reverence, obedience, and a God-hungry heart? To what do these practices lead in the end?

Marching Orders

1. Read 2 Samuel 6.

    A. Compare verses 1–7 with Numbers 4:15. What went wrong with this first attempt to move the ark? How could the tragedy have been prevented?

    B. How does the Bible describe David's conduct in verses 14, 16 and 20? What does this tell you about him?

    C. How does David respond to his wife's criticism in verses 21–22? What does this tell you about his character?

2. Read Matthew 28:18–20.
   A. Why can you be supremely confident that what Jesus gives you to do, you can accomplish (v. 18)?
   B. What part do you play in the task Jesus describes in verses 19–20?
   C. How does verse 20 make it clear that this promise and mission were not intended only for Jesus's first-century disciples?

3. Read Hebrews 10:22.
   A. What are we encouraged to do in this verse?
   B. How are we encouraged to do this?
   C. How are we able to do this?

Battle Lines

Many of us are so accustomed to the comforts of modern life that we fail to appreciate the magnificence of God's creation. To heighten your appreciation of the majesty and grandeur of God—and to gain a greater awe of his power—find a place far from city lights, and spend a few hours in the open countryside, taking in the majesty of a night sky. Count the stars, if you can, and remember that God created every one and calls them all by name. What an awesome God he is!

14

TOUGH PROMISES

Reconnaissance

1. A promise prompted David. The king is kind, not because the boy is deserving, but because the promise is enduring.
   A. What promises have meant the most to you over the years? Who made them? How did they keep them?

B. Why is an enduring promise so comforting? Would you say that your own promises are enduring? Explain.

2. God makes and never breaks his promises. The Hebrew word for covenant, *beriyth*, means "a solemn agreement with binding force." His irrevocable covenant runs like a scarlet thread through the tapestry of Scripture.
    A. How has God shown his commitment to keeping his promises in your life?
    B. How does it make you feel to know that God's promise provides the foundation for your salvation?

3. Your eternal life is covenant caused, covenant secured, and covenant based. You can put Lo Debar in the rearview mirror for one reason—God keeps his promises. Shouldn't God's promise keeping inspire yours?
    A. How would your life be different if God did *not* keep his promises?
    B. Why should God's promise keeping inspire your own commitment to keeping promises? Does it? Explain.

4. You're tired. You're angry. You're disappointed. This isn't the marriage you expected or the life you wanted. But looming in your past is a promise you made. May I urge you to do all you can to keep it? To give it one more try? Why should you? So you can understand the depth of God's love.
    A. Of the promises you've made, which seems most in jeopardy right now?
    B. How can keeping your promise help you to better understand and appreciate God's love for you?

5. When you love the unloving, you get a glimpse of what God does for you. When you keep the porch light on for the

prodigal child, when you do what is right even though you
have been done wrong, when you love the weak and the sick,
you do what God does every single moment.

    A. What "unloving" person(s) does God call you to love?

    B. Think back through the past week. How has God con-
tinued to demonstrate his love to you, despite unloving
actions on your part?

Marching Orders

1. Read 2 Samuel 9.

    A. What prompted David to ask about Saul's family?

    B. At first, what did Mephibosheth think about all this
new royal interest in him?

    C. How did David's actions help to set Mephibosheth's
heart at ease (v. 7)?

2. Read 2 Corinthians 1:20.

    A. How many of God's promises have passed their expira-
tion date?

    B. For whom are God's promises valid?

    C. How do we best honor God for keeping his promises?

3. Read 2 Peter 1:3–4.

    A. What do we lack in order to grow into mature
believers?

    B. What kind of promises have we been given?

    C. What do these promises enable us to do?

Battle Lines

The book of Genesis contains many of the most important covenants in the Bible. Take some time to study the following covenants,
keeping in mind your relationship to them: Genesis 6:18–22; 9:9–17;
15:18–19; 17:2–14, 19–21 (also see Exodus 2:24).

15

THIN AIR-OGANCE

Reconnaissance

1. David suffers from altitude sickness. He's been too high too long. The thin air has messed with his senses. He can't hear as he used to. He can't hear the warnings of the servant or the voice of his conscience. Nor can he hear his Lord. The pinnacle has dulled his ears and blinded his eyes.

   A. In your own words, how would you describe this kind of altitude sickness?

   B. When are you most in danger of suffering from this kind of altitude sickness?

2. How is your hearing? Do you hear the servants whom God sends? Do you hear the conscience that God stirs? And your vision? Do you still see people? Or do you see only their functions? Do you see people who need you, or do you see people beneath you?

   A. How would you answer each of Max's questions above?

   B. In what area of life may God be trying to get your attention right now?

3. David never quite recovered from this bout with this giant. Don't make his mistake. 'Tis far wiser to descend the mountain than fall from it.

   A. What do you think Max means when he writes, "'Tis far wiser to descend the mountain than fall from it"?

   B. What mountain may you need to descend voluntarily, at least for a time?

4. Pursue humility. . . . Embrace your poverty. . . . Resist the place of celebrity.

A. What would it look like for you to pursue humility?

B. What poverty do you have that you should embrace?

C. How can you best resist the place of celebrity?

Marching Orders

1. Read 2 Samuel 11:1–26.

   A. What was the start of David's problems in this chapter?

   B. How did Uriah—a Hittite, not a Hebrew—show himself to be far more honorable than David (v. 11)?

   C. How does this incident illustrate the truth of Numbers 32:23?

2. Read Proverbs 16:18.

   A. How does pride destroy a person?

   B. In what way did David show himself prideful in the incident with Bathsheba?

   C. What kind of destruction and fall did David experience when God revealed his sin?

3. Read 1 Peter 5:6.

   A. What command are believers given in this verse?

   B. What promise is given to those who heed the command?

   C. When will God fulfill this promise?

Battle Lines

Time after time in the Bible we are told to humble ourselves. In what area of life do you most need to humble yourself? Spend some time thinking about this, and then lay out a plan with specifics of how you can actually do it. Determine some practical, concrete steps you can take *this week* to humble yourself in this area. Then take them.

16

COLOSSAL COLLAPSES

Reconnaissance

1. David seduces—no mention of God. David plots—no mention of God. Uriah buried, Bathsheba married—no mention of God. God is not spoken to and does not speak.

   A. Do you think this absence of God is the cause or the result of what happened in David's life? Explain.

   B. Why do you think God does not speak to David during all this evil activity? Why is he silent?

2. God's words reflect hurt, not hate; bewilderment, not belittlement. Your flock fills the hills. Why rob? Beauty populates your palace. Why take from someone else?

   A. What do you think hurt God the most about David's sin?

   B. What do you think hurts God the most about your sin?

3. Colossal collapses won't leave us alone. They surface like a boil on the skin.

   A. Why do colossal collapses not leave us alone? Is this a good thing or a bad thing? Explain.

   B. Have you ever suffered a colossal collapse? If so, what steps did you take to recover from it?

4. You think my mom was tough . . . Try the hands of God. Unconfessed sins sit on our hearts like festering boils, poisoning, expanding. And God, with gracious thumbs, applies the pressure.

   A. If God knows everything, then why is it so tough sometimes to confess our sins to him?

B. How can grace sometimes cause such deep suffering?
How can pain ever be a gracious thing?

5. God did with David's sin what he does with yours and
mine—he put it away. It's time for you to put your "third
week of March 1987" to rest. Assemble a meeting of three
parties: you, God, and your memory. Place the mistake before
the judgment seat of God. Let him condemn it, let him pardon it, and let him put it away.

A. How does God's putting away a sin differ from merely
forgetting it?

B. Have you asked God to put away your sins—all of
them? Explain.

Marching Orders

1. Read 2 Samuel 11:27–12:25.

A. Name all the elements of David's behavior in this
passage that displeased the Lord.

B. How did the prophecy of 12:10 reach its culmination in
the life of Jesus Christ?

C. What was the first thing David did right after many
months of willful rebellion (12:13)? How did God
respond to him?

2. Read Psalm 32:3–5.

A. How did David feel during the time he tried to cover up
his sin?

B. How did God deal with David during the time he
refused to admit his sin?

C. How did God react when David finally confessed
his sin?

3. Read Psalm 103:11–13.

A. For whom does the Lord have great love, according to verse 11? What does it mean to fear God?
B. State the point of verse 12 in your own words.
C. On whom does the Lord shower great compassion, according to verse 13?

Battle Lines

Is there some sin in your recent past that you have yet to name, confess, and abandon? If there is, take time right now to get before the Lord and name that sin for what it is—spiritual rebellion, a slap in God's face, a dark stain on the holy person God has made you to be. Thank God that he has removed your guilt as far as the east is from the west, and ask him for strength not only to avoid that sin in the future but to gladly obey his counsel and his Word.

17

FAMILY MATTERS

Reconnaissance

1. Going AWOL on his family was David's greatest failure. His passive parenting and widespread philandering were not sins of a slothful afternoon or the deranged reactions of self-defense. David's family foul-up was a lifelong stupor that cost him dearly.
   A. Do you agree that going AWOL on his family was David's greatest failure? Why or why not?
   B. What, if anything, does David's handling of his family have in common with the way you handle your family?

2. David succeeded everywhere except at home. And if you don't succeed at home, do you succeed at all?

    A. How would you answer Max's question above?

    B. How does succeeding at home honor God?

3. On your wedding day, God loaned you his work of art: an intricately crafted, precisely formed masterpiece. He entrusted you with a one-of-a-kind creation. Value her. Honor him.

    A. If you are married, describe the work of art that God loaned you on your wedding day.

    B. How can you value your wife in practical, obvious ways? How can you honor your husband in concrete, satisfying ways?

4. Moms and dads, more valuable than all the executives and lawmakers west of the Mississippi, quietly hold the world together.

    A. Do you agree with the sentiment expressed above? If so, why? If not, why not?

    B. Describe the influence your mom and dad had on you.

5. I suspect that David would have traded all his conquered crowns for the tender arms of a wife. But it was too late. He died in the care of a stranger, because he made strangers out of his family. But it's not too late for you.

    A. What areas of your home would you like to see improve over the next year?

    B. What specific things can you do to encourage those improvements?

Marching Orders

1. Read 2 Samuel 13:21, 37–38; 14:28; 15:1–37; 1 Kings 1:6.

    A. What kind of father did David appear to be, based on the information in these verses?

    B. How did David fail as a husband?

    C.   What could David have done differently to spare him the family troubles he faced?

2.   Read Proverbs 25:28; 29:11; Acts 24:25.
   A.   Why is a man who lacks self-control like a city whose walls are broken down?
   B.   What is the biblical name for someone who refuses to control his or her temper?
   C.   Would you have expected Paul to include self-control as a topic along with righteousness and final judgment? Explain.

3.   Read Ephesians 6:4 and Titus 2:4–5.
   A.   Why do you think fathers (as opposed to mothers) are given the instruction of Ephesians 6:4?
   B.   Who is given the responsibility of teaching young mothers how to build a strong, godly home (Titus 2:4)?
   C.   What is the rationale behind this instruction (Titus 2:5)?

Battle Lines

Do you really want to know how healthy your family life is? Then start by taking a poll of your family members. Ask all of them individually how they feel about the way you treat them, the way you lead them, the way you care for them. Take these conversations seriously, make any corrections that seem necessary, offer any apologies that are needed, and commit to God to build the strongest family possible.

18

DASHED HOPES

Reconnaissance

1. I had intended . . . I had made preparations . . . *But* God . . .
   A. What does this story of David's desire to build the temple say to those who think that personal dreams are always the pathway to God's best?
   B. What plans have you made and prepared for that God altered somehow?

2. What do you do with the "but God" moments in life? When God interrupts your good plans, how do you respond?
   A. How do you answer the two questions above?
   B. Do you see these "but God" moments as good or bad? Explain.

3. When you are given an ice cream sundae, you don't complain over a missing cherry. David faced the behemoth of disappointment with "yet God." David trusted.
   A. Why do we often complain over a missing cherry when God gives us an ice cream sundae? Have you ever done this? If so, describe what happened.
   B. How have you trusted God in the disappointing moments of your life?

4. His "but God" became a "yet God." Who's to say yours won't become the same?
   A. What explains the transition from "but God" to "yet God"? What makes the difference?
   B. What "yet God" would you like to see overrun a "but God"? Describe it.

Marching Orders

1. Read 1 Chronicles 28:2–19.
   - A. What did David desire to do? Was this a good desire (see 2 Chronicles 6:8)?
   - B. Why did God not allow David to see his desire fulfilled?
   - C. What did God give David instead?

2. Read Acts 16:6–10.
   - A. Describe Paul's original travel plans. Was it good for him to have a plan?
   - B. How did God alter Paul's ministry plans? Why did he do this?
   - C. What happened when Paul allowed God to alter his plans?

3. Read Job 42:2; Proverbs 21:30; Jeremiah 29:11.
   - A. Why can we have confidence in God's plans for us?
   - B. Why do we not have to fear that someone else's plans will derail the future God has planned for us?
   - C. What kind of plan does God have for us, according to Jeremiah 29:11?

Battle Lines

Too often we make our plans and ask God to bless them rather than asking God to help us build our plans in a way that pleases him. Have you submitted your plans to God? If not, do so today. Pray something like this: "Father, I don't want to run in my own direction. I want to be where you want me to be, doing what you want me to do. So forgive me for making my plans without you, and help me to get on track with you. Show me your plans for my life, and then give me the courage and the wisdom to follow them. And, Lord, when I run into a 'but God,' help me to immediately start looking for the 'yet God.' In Jesus's name, Amen."

19

TAKE GOLIATH DOWN!

Reconnaissance

Use your five fingers to remind you of the five stones you need to face down your Goliath. Let your thumb remind you of . . .

1. The stone of the past

Catalog God's successes. Keep a list of his world records. Has he not walked you through high waters? Proven to be faithful? Have you not known his provision? . . . Write today's worries in sand. Chisel yesterday's victories in stone.

    A.   In the past year, what successes has God given you? Throughout your Christian life, what high waters has he walked you through?

    B.   Think about the last month. Which worries that occupied your time never materialized?

2. The stone of prayer

Note the valley between your thumb and finger. To pass from one to the next you must go through it. Let it remind you of David's descent. Before going high, David went low; before ascending to fight, David descended to prepare. Don't face your giant without first doing the same. Dedicate time to prayer.

    A.   What sorts of things do you normally pray about? What sorts of things seem to escape your notice in prayer?

    B.   When is the best time for you to pray? Why?

3. The stone of priority

Let your tallest finger remind you of your highest priority: God's reputation.

    A. If God's reputation were based solely on your behavior, what kind of reputation would God have?

    B. If you were to live all of life for God's glory—including your family life, your work life, your recreational life, and so forth—what would need to change?

4. The stone of passion

David ran, not away from, but toward his giant. . . . Do the same! What good has problem pondering gotten you? You've stared so long you can number the hairs on Goliath's chest. Has it helped? No. Listing hurts won't heal them. Itemizing problems won't solve them. Categorizing rejections won't remove them. David lobotomized the giant because he emphasized the Lord.

    A. What are you most passionate about? Would you say you are passionate about God? Explain.

    B. How could you increase your passion for God? What could you do to move him toward the top spot in your life?

5. The stone of persistence

Never give up. One prayer might not be enough. One apology might not do it. One day or month of resolve might not suffice. You may get knocked down a time or two . . . but don't quit. Keep loading the rocks. Keep swinging the sling.

    A. How has a lack of persistence hurt you in the past? How has a commitment to persistence paid off so far?

B. Who is the most persistent person you know? What gives him or her this quality? What can you learn from this person to increase your own persistence?

Marching Orders

1. Read 1 Chronicles 16:7–36.
   A. Why is it so important to speak of what God has done?
   B. Why is it so important to remember the covenant oaths God has made?
   C. Why is it so important to worship God with a grateful and exuberant heart?

2. Read Ephesians 6:18–20.
   A. What does it mean to pray "in the Spirit"?
   B. For whom are we instructed to pray? How often?
   C. Why is it important to stay alert in our prayers?

3. Read Colossians 3:23–24.
   A. Regardless of your employer, whom do you really work for? Why is this important to remember?
   B. Why does God consider it so important that we go about our business with all our hearts?
   C. What reward is promised to those who comply with this command?

Battle Lines

Throughout the Bible, and still today, God is looking for those who will be wholehearted about whatever they do, as they pursue it for his glory. Do a self-inventory. In what areas of life are you wholehearted? In what areas of life are you less than wholehearted? How can you submit all of life to the lordship of Christ and live passionately in every arena?

AFTERWORD

WHAT BEGAN IN BETHLEHEM

Reconnaissance

1. Seems you, like David, have much in common with Jesus. Big deal? I think so. Jesus understands you. He understands small-town anonymity and big-city pressure. He's walked pastures of sheep and palaces of kings. He's faced hunger, sorrow, and death and wants to face them with you.
   A. What do you think you have in common with Jesus? List several items.
   B. How can Jesus help you face hunger, sorrow, and death?

2. Jesus never missed the mark. Equally amazing, he never distances himself from those who do.
   A. Why is it important that Jesus never missed the mark?
   B. How can Jesus be an example for you in dealing with difficult people?

3. Jesus wasn't ashamed of David. He isn't ashamed of you. He calls you brother; he calls you sister. The question is, do you call him Savior?
   A. Why wasn't Jesus ashamed of David? Why isn't he ashamed of you?
   B. Do you call Jesus your Savior? Explain.

4. One word from you, and God will do again what he did with David and millions like him: he'll claim you, save you, and use you.
   A. What difference does it make to you that God has claimed you for his own?

    B.   How do you think God wants to use you? What mission has he assigned you?

Marching Orders

1. Read Hebrews 4:14–16.

    A.   Why should having Jesus as our great high priest better enable us to "hold firmly to the faith we profess" (NIV)?

    B.   How is Jesus able to understand our weaknesses?

    C.   How is our great high priest different from us?

2. Read 1 John 4:9–11.

    A.   How did God show his love for us? What was the purpose of this action (v. 9)?

    B.   Why did Jesus come into this world, according to verse 10?

    C.   What conclusion does John reach, based on what he has said in verses 9–10?

3. Read Hebrews 2:11–18.

    A.   According to verse 11, what does Jesus call those he saves? Why does he call them this?

    B.   What was the purpose for Jesus becoming human, according to verses 14–15?

    C.   Why can Jesus fully understand any problem or challenge you face, according to verses 17–18? How does this make him the perfect helper for you?

Battle Lines

Spend some time thanking God for claiming you, saving you, and using you. Ask him to use you to bring others to him, and then look for ways to bless others as God has blessed you. Review the five stones with which you've been equipped to face your giants.

NOTES

Chapter 1: Facing Your Giants
1. Author's paraphrase.
2. See Exodus 9:22–23; Joshua 6:15–20; 1 Samuel 7:10.
3. Author's paraphrase.
4. Emphasis mine in this list of scriptures.

Chapter 3: Raging Sauls
1. Attributed to George Eliot.
2. Names and details have been changed.

Chapter 4: Desperate Days
1. Eugene H. Peterson, *Leap Over a Wall: Earthy Spirituality for Everyday Christians* (San Francisco: HarperSanFrancisco, 1997), 65.

Chapter 5: Dry Seasons
1. Malachi Martin, *King of Kings* (New York: Simon and Schuster, 1980), 206.
2. "Reinstated," *Favorite Stories from Bob Russell,* vol. 5, CD-ROM (Louisville, KY: Living Word, Inc., 2005).

Notes

Chapter 6: Grief-Givers

1. http://www.oklahomacitynationalmemorial.org/media
2. M. Norville Young with Mary Hollingsworth, *Living Lights, Shining Stars: Ten Secrets to Becoming the Light of the World* (West Monroe, LA: Howard Publishing, 1997), 39.

Chapter 7: Barbaric Behavior

1. Ernest Gordon, *To End All Wars: A True Story About the Will to Survive and the Courage to Forgive* (Grand Rapids: Zondervan, 2002), 105–6, 101.
2. Hans Wilhelm Hertzberg, *I and II Samuel*, trans. J. S. Bowden (Philadelphia: Westminster Press, 1964), 199–200.
3. Gordon, *To End All Wars*, 101–2.

Chapter 8: Slump Guns

1. Associated Press, "450 Sheep Jump to their Deaths in Turkey," July 8, 2005.
2. C. J. Mahaney, "Loving the Church," audiotape of message at Covenant Life Church, Gaithersburg, MD, n.d., quoted in Randy Alcorn, *Heaven* (Wheaton, IL: Tyndale House, 2004), xxii.

Chapter 9: Plopping Points

1. Peterson, *Leap Over a Wall*, 112.

Chapter 10: Unspeakable Grief

1. C. S. Lewis, *A Grief Observed* (San Francisco: HarperSanFrancisco, 1961), 24.
2. F. B. Meyer, *Abraham*, quoted in Charles R. Swindoll, *The Tale of the Tardy Oxcart: And 1,501 Other Stories* (Nashville: Word Publishing, 1998), 254.
3. Ann Kaiser Stearns, *Living Through Personal Crisis* (New York: Ballantine Books, 1984), 6.
4. Thomas P. Davidson, *I Called Him Roosk, He Called Me Dad: A Collection of Thoughts About a Father's Faith, Love, and Grief After Losing His Son* (privately printed), 36–37.

Notes

Chapter 11: Blind Intersections

1. George Arthur Butterick, ed., *The Interpreter's Dictionary of the Bible: An Illustrated Encyclopedia,* (Nashville: Abingdon, 1962), s.v. "Urim and Thummin," and Merrill C. Tenney, gen. ed., *Pictorial Bible Dictionary* (Nashville: Southwestern Company, 1975), s.v. "Urim and Thummim."

2. F. B. Meyer. *David: Shepherd, Psalmist, King* (Fort Washington, PA: Christian Literature Crusade, 1977), 101–2.

Chapter 13: Distant Deity

1. Some scholars suggest that "sons of Abinadab" in 2 Samuel 6:3 should be understood in the broader sense of "descendants of Abinadab" (Earl D. Radmacher, gen. ed., *Nelson's New Illustrated Bible Commentary* [Nashville: Thomas Nelson Inc., 1999]). See also 1 Samuel 7:1, where Eleazar is called Abinadab's son.

Chapter 14: Tough Promises

1. Fred Lowery, *Covenant Marriage: Staying Together for Life* (West Monroe, LA: Howard Publishing, 2002), 44.

2. Lowery, *Covenant Marriage,* 45.

Chapter 16: Colossal Collapses

1. *San Antonio Express News,* "Does Texan have a prayer of trading domain name?" April 23, 2005.

Chapter 18: Dashed Hopes

1. Paul Aurandt, *Paul Harvey's the Rest of the Story,* ed. and comp. Lynne Harvey (New York: Bantam Books, 1978), 107–9.

Chapter 19: Taking Goliath Down!

1. The offering exceeded our expectations.

Other *Facing Your Giants* Products

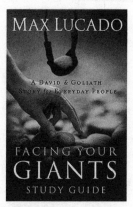

Everyone has a "*Goliath*"—a problem so overwhelming it is seemingly gigantesque in its magnitude. *Facing Your Giants Study Guide* has the answers that believers need in order to face the giants in life. Whether your overwhelming problem is grief that you just can't deal with, divorce that has ravaged your family, or an addiction that has a vice-like clamp on your willpower, *Facing Your Giants Study Guide* will teach you to look past your problem towards the solution. Based on the life of David, this study guide is guaranteed to provide inspiration to succeed against even the most threatening difficulty.

Listen to the message of *Facing Your Giants* in your home or take it on the road. This CD makes the perfect gift for the family or friends you know are struggling to face their giants.

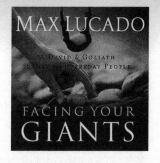

Facing Your Giants is also available in Spanish and Portuguese

GRUPO NELSON
Desde 1798

Para otros materiales, visítenos a:
gruponelson.com

The Lucado Reader's Guide

Discover . . . Inside every book by Max Lucado, you'll find words of encouragement and inspiration that will draw you into a deeper experience with Jesus and treasures for your walk with God. What will you discover?

3:16: The Numbers of Hope
. . . the 26 words that can change your life.
core scripture: John 3:16

And the Angels Were Silent
. . . what Jesus Christ's final days can teach you about what matters most.
core scripture: Matthew 20–27

The Applause of Heaven
. . . the secret to a truly satisfying life.
core scripture: The Beatitudes, Matthew 5:1–10

Come Thirsty
. . . how to rehydrate your heart and sink into the wellspring of God's love.
core scripture: John 7:37–38

Cure for the Common Life
. . . the unique things God designed you to do with your life.
core scripture: 1 Corinthians 12:7

Facing Your Giants
. . . when God is for you, no challenge is too great.
core scripture: 1 and 2 Samuel

Fearless
. . . how faith is the antidote to the fear in your life.
core scripture: John 14:1, 3

A Gentle Thunder
. . . the God who will do whatever it takes to lead his children back to Him.
core scripture: Psalm 81:7

Great Day Every Day
. . . how living in a purposeful way will help you trust more, stress less.
core scripture: Psalm 118:24

The Great House of God
. . . a blueprint for peace, joy, and love found in the Lord's Prayer.
core scripture: The Lord's Prayer, Matthew 6:9–13

God Came Near
. . . a love so great that it left heaven to become part of your world.
core scripture: John 1:14

He Chose the Nails
. . . a love so deep that it chose death on a cross—just to win your heart.
core scripture: 1 Peter 1:18–20

He Still Moves Stones
. . . the God who still does the impossible—in your life.
core scripture: Matthew 12:20

In the Eye of the Storm
. . . peace in the storms of your life.
core scripture: John 6

In the Grip of Grace
. . . the greatest gift of all—the grace of God.
core scripture: Romans

It's Not About Me
. . . why focusing on God will make sense of your life.
core scripture: 2 Corinthians 3:18

Just Like Jesus
. . . a life free from guilt, fear, and anxiety.
core scripture: Ephesians 4:23–24

A Love Worth Giving
. . . how living loved frees you to love others.
core scripture: 1 Corinthians 13

Next Door Savior
. . . a God who walked life's hardest trials—and still walks with you through yours.
core scripture: Matthew 16:13–16

No Wonder They Call Him the Savior
. . . hope in the unlikeliest place— upon the cross.
core scripture: Romans 5:15

Outlive Your Life
. . . that a great God created you to do great things.
core scripture: Acts 1

Six Hours One Friday
. . . forgiveness and healing in the middle of loss and failure.
core scripture: John 19–20

Traveling Light
. . . the power to release the burdens you were never meant to carry.
core scripture: Psalm 23

When God Whispers Your Name
. . . the path to hope in knowing that God knows you, never forgets you, and cares about the details of your life.
core scripture: John 10:3

When Christ Comes
. . . why the best is yet to come.
core scripture: 1 Corinthians 15:23

Recommended reading if you're struggling with . . .

FEAR AND WORRY
Come Thirsty
Fearless
For the Tough Times
Next Door Savior
Traveling Light

DISCOURAGEMENT
He Still Moves Stones
Next Door Savior

GRIEF/DEATH OF A LOVED ONE
Next Door Savior
Traveling Light
When Christ Comes
When God Whispers Your Name

GUILT
In the Grip of Grace
Just Like Jesus

LONELINESS
God Came Near

SIN
Facing Your Giants
He Chose the Nails
Six Hours One Friday

WEARINESS
When God Whispers Your Name

Recommended reading if you want to know more about . . .

THE CROSS
And the Angels Were Silent
He Chose the Nails
No Wonder They Call Him the Savior
Six Hours One Friday

GRACE
He Chose the Nails
In the Grip of Grace

HEAVEN
The Applause of Heaven
When Christ Comes

SHARING THE GOSPEL
God Came Near
No Wonder They Call Him the Savior

Recommended reading if you're looking for more . . .

COMFORT
For the Tough Times
He Chose the Nails
Next Door Savior
Traveling Light

COMPASSION
Outlive Your Life

COURAGE
Facing Your Giants
Fearless

HOPE
3:16: The Numbers of Hope
Facing Your Giants
A Gentle Thunder
God Came Near

JOY
The Applause of Heaven
Cure for the Common Life
When God Whispers Your Name

LOVE
Come Thirsty
A Love Worth Giving
No Wonder They Call Him the Savior

PEACE
And the Angels Were Silent
The Great House of God
In the Eye of the Storm
Traveling Light

SATISFACTION
And the Angels Were Silent
Come Thirsty
Cure for the Common Life
Every Day Deserves a Chance

TRUST
A Gentle Thunder
It's Not About Me
Next Door Savior

Max Lucado books make great gifts!
If you're coming up to a special occasion, consider one of these.

FOR ADULTS:
For the Tough Times
Grace for the Moment
Live Loved
The Lucado Life Lessons Study Bible
Mocha with Max
DaySpring Daybrighteners® and cards

FOR TEENS/GRADUATES:
Let the Journey Begin
You Can Be Everything God Wants You to Be
You Were Made to Make a Difference

FOR KIDS:
Just in Case You Ever Wonder
The Oak Inside the Acorn
You Are Special

FOR PASTORS AND TEACHERS:
God Thinks You're Wonderful
You Changed My Life

AT CHRISTMAS:
The Crippled Lamb
Christmas Stories from Max Lucado
God Came Near

THE CAMPAIGN TO MAKE
POVERTY HISTORY
WWW.ONE.ORG

There is a plague of biblical proportions taking place in Africa right now, but we can beat this crisis, if we each do our part. Step ONE is signing the ONE petition, to join the ONE Campaign.

The ONE Campaign is a new effort to rally Americans—ONE by ONE—to fight global AIDS and extreme poverty. We are engaging Americans everywhere we gather—in churches and synagogues, on the internet and college campuses, at community meetings and concerts. To learn more about The ONE Campaign, go to www.one.org and sign the online petition.

"Use your uniqueness to take great risks for God! If you're great with kids, volunteer at the orphanage. If you have a head for business, start a soup kitchen. If God bent you toward medicine, dedicate a day or a decade to AIDS patients. The only mistake is not to risk making one."

—Max Lucado, *Cure for the Common Life*

ONE Voice can make a difference.
Let God work through you; join the ONE Campaign now!

This campaign is brought to you by

Inspired by what you just read?

Connect with Max.

Listen to Max's teaching ministry, UpWords, on the radio and online. Visit www.MaxLucado.com to get FREE resources for spiritual growth and encouragement, including:

- Archives of UpWords, Max's daily radio program, and a list of radio stations where it airs
- Devotionals and e-mails from Max
- First look at book excerpts
- Downloads of audio, video, and printed material
- Mobile content

You will also find an online store and special offers.

www.MaxLucado.com

1-800-822-9673

UpWords Ministries
P.O. Box 692170
San Antonio, TX 78269-2170

Join the Max Lucado community:

Follow Max on Twitter @MaxLucado
or at Facebook.com/UpWordsMinistry